This book is dedicated to four people. First, to all my *J*'s: my wife, Joan, who sustained me through the writing; my son John, who checked my logic; and my son James, who reminded me that sometimes play is more important than writing. Second, to Robert Holmes who taught me much about peace, both academically and through his interactions with students and colleagues.

What about Hitler?

The Christian Practice of Everyday Life

David S. Cunningham
and William T. Cavanaugh, series editors

This series seeks to present specifically Christian perspectives on some of the most prevalent contemporary practices of everyday life. It is intended for a broad audience—including clergy, interested laypeople, and students. The books in this series are motivated by the conviction that, in the contemporary context, Christians must actively demonstrate that their allegiance to the God of Jesus Christ always takes priority over secular structures that compete for our loyalty—including the state, the market, race, class, gender, and other functional idolatries. The books in this series will examine these competing allegiances as they play themselves out in particular day-to-day practices, and will provide concrete descriptions of how the Christian faith might play a more formative role in our everyday lives.

The Christian Practice of Everyday Life series is an initiative of The Ekklesia Project, an ecumenical gathering of pastors, theologians, and lay leaders committed to helping the church recall its status as the distinctive, real-world community dedicated to the priorities and practices of Jesus Christ and to the inbreaking Kingdom of God. (For more information on The Ekklesia Project, see <www.ekklesiaproject.org>.)

What about Hitler?

Wrestling with Jesus's Call to Nonviolence in an Evil World

THE CHRISTIAN PRACTICE OF
EVERYDAY LIFE Series

Robert W. Brimlow

Brazos Press
Grand Rapids, Michigan

© 2006 by Robert W. Brimlow

Published by Brazos Press
a division of Baker Publishing Group
P.O. Box 6287, Grand Rapids, MI 49516-6287
www.brazospress.com

Printed in the United States of America

Library of Congress Cataloging-in-Publication Data
Brimlow, Robert W., 1954–
    What about Hitler? : wrestling with Jesus's call to nonviolence in an evil world / Robert W. Brimlow.
        p.   cm. — (the Christian practice of everyday life)
    Includes bibliographical references.
    ISBN 10: 1-58743-065-7 (pbk.)
    ISBN 978-1-58743-065-7 (pbk.)
    1. Nonviolence—Religious aspects—Christianity. 2. Peace—Religious aspects—Christianity.
I. Title. II. Series.
BT736.6.B75 2006
241'.6242—dc22   2006004075

All Scripture is taken from THE NEW JERUSALEM BIBLE, copyright © 1985 by Darton, Longman & Todd, Ltd. and Doubleday, a division of Bantam Doubleday Dell Publishing Group, Inc. Reprinted by permission.

Contents

Revelation does not deal with the mystery of God, but with the life of man. And it deals with the life of man as that which can and should be lived in the face of the mystery of God, and turning toward that mystery, even more, the life of man *is* so lived, when it is his true life.

—Martin Buber

Preface

■ This book has an interesting genesis. A number of years ago when I was a member of the Ekklesia Project, another member of that group sent an e-mail to a number of us asking, essentially, how Christian pacifists should respond to objections centering on fighting in World War II. I don't recall if the writer actually posed the question, "Well, what about Hitler?" but the effect was the same.

I had come to term it "the Hitler question" for a number of years prior to that e-mail. Whenever I would make an argument in favor of pacifism in my philosophy classes or when addressing an audience, inevitably someone would ask me the Hitler question. Invariably I would come up with some kind of answer, and invariably I would not be especially happy with it. There was always something about my response that was too facile or fundamentally inadequate, primarily because deep down I knew that, if I had the chance, I would probably have killed Hitler using any means possible.

I never considered it good form for a pacifist to admit such a thing, so I never did. But the apparent disconnect between what I believe and what I would do troubled me whenever I thought about it. So I didn't think about it much.

I read the responses to the e-mailed question with a lot of interest. They were all necessarily brief, and since they were written by folks who are much wiser than I, they contained fascinating nuggets that began to help me clarify my own thoughts. Something was missing, however, and I thought it was due to the brevity of the responses.

Early in 2001 I submitted a proposal for a book on this topic in which a number of theologians and other Christian thinkers would answer the Hitler question—how would Christian peacemaking respond to the kind of evil-doing that Hitler represents? The editors of the series thought the idea was a fine one, but they also thought that the book would be more interesting and effective if it were written by a single author. They asked me to revise the proposal accordingly.

I am afraid I was both flattered and panicky. I was flattered that they thought I could write this book, but I was panicky because I didn't know what to say. I was still painfully aware of my ambivalence and had been looking forward to editing the collection of essays as a rescue mission. I am not sure why, but I agreed to give it a shot, and by June of 2001 my revised proposal was accepted.

Then came September 11, 2001.

After September 11, what had been in my mind an abstract and rather remote problem for Christian pacifists suddenly became concrete and very present. Many of us counseled peace even as we shared in the grief, anger, and fear, but I do not know how well our voices were heard in the tumult of those days. My own experiences were less than pleasant in that I often evoked an angry response. The worst, however, was one venue where an audience of over a hundred people met my remarks with silence. For some reason, that reaction frightened me more than the anger. But over time, with prayer and thought, my ambivalence began to recede.

It is difficult to write a book on peacemaking during a time of war, when war appears to be the only answer. Suddenly, after that September, the book developed in me a sense of urgency and responsibility to which I am unaccustomed, being an academic. I wrote and discarded numerous drafts and further outlines until it dawned on me that it was beyond my capabilities to write the kind of book that would answer all objections or be the kind of book that anyone would find plausible. Fundamentally, what I have to say in the book is absurd, and once I admitted that to myself, the writing of it became a little bit easier.

That is an odd claim to put in a preface, especially by a philosopher who, ostensibly anyway, makes his living by being rational and convincing. Even if I have written this well, that is, clearly, adequately reasoned and expressed—which I am not sure I have—the best reaction I can hope for is that some readers will call it implausible and unrealistic. I understand fully, I think, just what those kinds of objections mean, precisely because they have arisen within me as well. This book has taken me an inordinate amount of time to write, precisely because I struggled throughout to make my claims and arguments rational, plausible, and realistic; to take full account of who we Christians are, while recognizing our position in this country and as actors in the world.

That is what I have been struggling with and what I continue to struggle with. The problem is, essentially and in the clearest terms I can think of, that our call to follow Christ—what the call to discipleship means in the concrete—is unrealistic, implausible, and absurd. Ultimately I come back to Søren Kierkegaard. The idea of what we are called to be is in part so distasteful and unnatural to us that it seems to me that through most of our history our theologians and philosophers have spent much of their time and effort explaining why Jesus could not have meant what he most clearly said. At the very least, this is true with regard to war and violence.

At the risk of putting it too negatively, part of what is entailed by our call to follow Jesus is that we are called away from violence. We are not called to be pacifists; we are called to be Christians, and part of what it means to be Christian is to be peacemakers. I will not develop the entire theology of this position in this book; but it is important for us to have the same starting point, so I will say a few words about this claim.

The gospel is full of teachings that counsel us to make peace by following Jesus, and there are numerous examples from the Lord's life that illustrate what those counsels mean. The problem is that those counsels and teachings and examples are very clear while, at the same time, they appear to be impossible. What makes them hard is not that they are too vague or so broadly expressed that they are open to a wide variety of contrary interpretations. They are straightforward and unambiguous. So why do they seem impossible?

Let's examine a few examples.

One of the more contentious teachings that we will look at more closely in the first chapter is from Matthew 5:38–41, where Jesus says,

> You have heard how it was said: *Eye for eye and tooth for tooth.* But I say this to you: offer no resistance to the wicked. On the contrary, if anyone hits you on the right cheek, offer him the other as well; if someone wishes to go to law with you to get your tunic, let him have your cloak as well.

And at Matthew 5:43-48, Jesus continues:

> You have heard how it was said *You will love your neighbour* and hate your enemy. But I say this to you, love your enemies and pray for those who persecute you; so that you may be children of your Father in heaven, for he

causes his sun to rise on the bad as well as the good. . . . For if you love those who love you, what reward will you get? Do not even the tax collectors do as much? And if you save your greetings for your brothers, are you doing anything exceptional? Do not even the gentiles do as much? You must therefore be perfect, just as your heavenly Father is perfect.

In Luke 6:27, Jesus reiterates this message with some variation:

But this day I say to you who are listening: love your enemies, do good to those who hate you, bless those who curse you, pray for those who treat you badly.

And, finally, from Mark 12:29–31:

Jesus replied, "This is the first [commandment]: *Listen, Israel, the Lord our God is the one, only Lord, and you must love the Lord your God with all your heart, with all your soul,* with all your mind *and with all your strength.* The second is this: You must love your neighbor as yourself. There is no commandment greater than these."

There are more quotes and texts, but these are sufficient. If anyone is interested in full-throated theological arguments in support of my contention that being a disciple of Christ involves being a peacemaker, the works of John Howard Yoder, Jacques Ellul, and Stanley Hauerwas contain some of the best. At base, though, this is what Jesus taught, so why do we find it impossible? Part of it, I think, centers around Jesus's teaching that is contained above in Matthew: "You must be perfect, just as your heavenly Father is perfect."

There is a wonderful priest who works at St. John Fisher College who shared a story with me. Some years ago he was teaching a religion class in a high school for boys and told his students that Christians were called to be pacifists. A student asked him what he would do if the student got up and punched him in the nose. Father responded that he would knock him into the next county; while it is true that Jesus taught us to turn the other cheek, Father explained that he had not attained that level of holiness yet. He was trying to be a good Christian, but he knew he would probably fail if struck. That level of honesty makes me envious. Of course I would hit you back, and of course I would be wrong. You must not allow my inability to live faithfully let you think that Jesus did not mean it.

So much of the gospel seems to ask us to do what we cannot do, things that run against human nature, like selling all and giving it to the poor, not having lust in our hearts, and, yes, loving enemies and turning our cheeks. Even the most basic of the commandments—to acknowledge God alone as the one and only Lord and to love him totally—is so hard as to seem impossible. Most days it seems as though we have many gods—family, work, and football, to name a few. And to rely on God for strength and sustenance runs counter to all we have been taught. Perhaps more so in this American culture than elsewhere, but I have been schooled to be self-reliant and self-sufficient, to carry my weaknesses very quietly if I admit them at all, and to ask for help only in extremis.

Over the years I have joined this attitude with one of self-importance. What I do matters to the fate of the world, and if I don't do something, then it will not get done. As my focus centers more and more upon me, there does not seem to be that much room for God, except as an after-thought or as a consolation once I fail; and when I fail, I am sure to share the blame with him.

I don't know if these attitudes of self-reliance and self-importance are culturally induced or are part of human nature. I just know they are present in me and around me. When I think on them, many times I am reminded of what an old Italian grandmother used to say in the neighborhood where I grew up: "The zebra. She can no change her spots." I am what I am, and we are what we are; it does no good to strive for perfection, because we can never attain it.

We Christians cannot change our spots either. The message I hope this book ultimately conveys is the message of the gospel—for us to change and be perfect, we need the help of the Lord and his body, the church. While our recognition that we are called to be disciples might occur suddenly, the transformation that is required takes time. The way to become faithful is to live faithfully. And regarding the specific topic this book focuses on, Christian peacemaking makes sense and ceases to be absurd only when it is embedded in a life of faithfulness and the practices that arise from our faithfulness. What I try to do at the end of this book is point out some ways that Christians can start to live faithfully, and I do that by looking at our tradition and examining the spiritual and corporal works of mercy. But it takes a while for me to get there.

It might seem curious that many of the early chapters of this book do not mention Jesus. When it came time for me to actually sit down and try to write this, I decided to do two things. First, I wanted to write a nonacademic book; and, second, I wanted to address my remarks to the church where it is, not to some ideal, mental vision of the church as it might one day be.

Two things flowed from those decisions. In the first place, I am an academic, and I discovered that even when I tried to write nonacademically, it came out true to my training. I have tried to moderate this tendency by addressing what I think is intellectually interesting and avoiding what I see to be academic minutiae, but we must remember the story of zebras and spots. In the second place, since I am trying to address the church where it is, when the church talks of war, talk of Jesus doesn't often come up. Even though just war theory has its genesis in the theology of St. Augustine, it has become fundamentally a secular doctrine, and it is that doctrine that the church utilizes most often in its thinking on warfare. In fact, I argue that this must be so, because no Christian could justify war without leaving Jesus and the gospel out of it.

There are two other features to this book that I need to address as well. There were times in the history of the church when Christian authors and thinkers would frame their works as prayers directed to God rather than words directed to believers. In fact, some of the monuments of Christian theology and philosophy, like St. Augustine's *Confessions* and St. Anselm's *Proslogion,* were written as prayers. That practice seems to have fallen out of favor, and that is unfortunate, because the amount of truthfulness we display before God tends to be greater than the amount we display to each other. I also reflected that one of my aims in the book was to stress the importance of prayer in a Christian's life and to talk about the honesty one is forced to live when one prays truthfully. Rather than talk about it, then, I decided that I would pray in this book. As is my practice, I pray several times a day and before beginning work. I recorded some of my pertinent meditations on scripture and include one before each chapter, editing only for some additional coherence and language usage. They are neither polemic nor apologetic but honest approaches to and interactions with the Lord. They, therefore, present a record of my complaints, confusion, and reluctance, and they often display ambivalence and insecurity and not a lot of consolation. In many ways I am as uncomfortable as I would be were I to publish love letters, but being comfortable is certainly not what being a disciple is about, so it seems to be a foolish reason not to include them.

At the beginning of each chapter I also include a small prologue. Many of these are ordinary reflections on ordinary episodes in my life and in history. By writing them, I hope to form a context for the chapters that will place the intellectual endeavor more concretely in our experience.

First Meditation

Luke 4:5–13

Then, leading him to a height, the devil showed him in a moment of time all the kingdoms of the world and said to him, "I will give you all this power and their splendour, for it has been handed over to me, for me to give it to anyone I choose. Do homage, then, to me, and it shall all be yours." But Jesus answered him, "Scripture says:

You must do homage to the Lord your God, him alone you must serve."

Then he led him to Jerusalem and set him on the parapet of the Temple. "If you are Son of God," he said to him, "throw yourself down from here for Scripture says:

He has given his angels orders about you to guard you
and again:
They will carry you in their arms in case you trip over a stone."

But Jesus answered him, "Scripture says:
Do not put the Lord your God to the test."

Having exhausted every way of putting him to the test, the devil left him until the opportune moment.

■ Lord, help me remember I am always in your presence.

Lord, I am beginning this book with the account of the beginning of your ministry. If it's true that we are called to live our lives the way you lived yours, then it strikes me that we will probably be subject to the same kinds of temptations you experienced and be pulled in directions we ought not to go. As I pray this passage, I am worried about the subtlety and the attractiveness of the alternatives to discipleship and even more by how those alternatives can come to seem right in line with what you ask of us.

First of all, I am not sure about the devil's strategy here. Why did he wait? If I were to tempt you, Lord, knowing that you would be fasting and praying for forty days in the desert, I think I would prefer to come at you around day twenty—the midpoint, when you must have been pretty hungry already and still had nearly three weeks to go. By approaching you near the end of your ordeal, I think the devil erred, because by then you must have regained the hope that you could finish and would be finally allowing yourself to look forward to a beer and a sandwich, or a cup of wine and a bowl of lentils, or whatever it was that you'd eat after a fast.

But in any event, I'm not sure how wise it is for me to sit here and wonder about the best way to tempt you, though well you know I am not averse to trying to tempt you myself with all sorts of deals, bargains, and exchanges that you never seem to go for. So instead, let's go into what was in your mind when you decided to have no part of the devil's deal. (By the way, not to second-guess the devil, the evangelist, or anyone else involved in this text, but I'm skipping the first temptation, because I think it's rather a foolish one. After all, it must have occurred to you on your own that you could turn stones into loaves of bread much earlier than this—like day nine?—and the fast is nearly over by this point anyway, so why would you blow it with food now? That first one strikes me as hardly a temptation at all.)

It's with the second temptation that I begin to get curious because it seems so odd to me. It exhibits such a different understanding of things than what I am accustomed to. The devil shows you all the kingdoms and nations of the world and declares *his* ownership of them. I'm not sure why you or the Father gave it all to him in the first place, or allowed him to take it and didn't at least hold the mortgage or something. In any case, what am I supposed to make of this? *All* the nations of the world in their power and splendor belong to the devil. I guess even Vatican City. So this doesn't leave me very many options, it seems, for political involvement; I can do without the splendor, but the power is something else again. Are you trying to tell me that *no* involvement with political power is permitted, or are you only trying to warn me away from excessive involvement and reliance on the states? I don't know, Lord. The way these verses read makes it difficult for me to understand how I can have anything to do with the nations, and you certainly do not make it any easier for me to figure out how I am supposed to follow you when you inspire Paul to write Romans 13 on top of this, either.

I am stuck here, maybe because I do not want to admit what you seem to be saying, so let's move on a bit.

The devil holds all of the earthly nations and their power in his possession and offers them back to you in exchange for homage. I am aware that some translations replace "homage" with "worship," but as my Greek has rusted from disuse, I'll accept this word. I also understand your refusal here, but before we get to that, this does seem to be such a pretty good deal that's it's hard for me to see it as a temptation: what an opportunity for evangelization! To paraphrase that great theologian and philosopher Lyndon Baines Johnson, if you've got them by their ears, their hearts and minds will follow.

So I look at this opportunity and see all the good that would follow. If all the political and economic power of the nations is yours, poverty is gone and all people can be well fed; welfare ends and we can get some decent health insurance. All of the ills that have befallen us, your brothers and sisters, could have been replaced with variations of days at the beach with ice cream. And think of the children you could have saved from all sorts of misery and exploitation, all for the price of a little homage that I don't think you would even have to mean deep inside.

I think I would go for this deal, Lord. You know better than I the homage I pay to the devil for so much less. So, give me this chance, and I think I'd take it. Why isn't the amount of good I could do with the power worth it, especially since I am in such a sorry state of soul anyway?

You say no to him, even if we translate it as *homage*—a paying of respect—instead of *worship*. It doesn't even seem as though you pause before answering that we must pay homage to the Lord our God and serve him alone. I do not want to serve the devil; I want to serve your people. And as soon as I write that, I know that is not what I am to do. Homage and worship to you; service to you, and I guess the rest follows. I don't like this much. I am usually awfully unsure what serving you means or how it is that I serve you by serving your people if serving your people is not enough.

Back to the text, the first refuge of the theologically unsure. This last temptation has me stumped, too. I wonder why you lead me to Luke's account instead of Matthew's. Matthew's ends with the offer of the nations' power, whereas Luke's ends with this strange scene. Why in the world would you want to throw yourself off the temple roof? If safety were the point, it would make more sense just to hang on. So I'm not clear just how this is a temptation or why you would want me to consider it third.

The only way I understand what is going on here is through your response that we should not put God to the test. But why not? There you are, up the tree, so to speak, without a paddle, and just having passed on all the power of the world, to boot, and all for the sake of God, so why shouldn't you call on God to help you? How is this a test and, even if it is a test, so what? If God doesn't help you in this situation, no one else will either, if for no other reason than that no one who cares about you is up on that roof and able to carry you down. If we are supposed to rely on God, how do we do that without putting him to the test? Or is our reliance on God operative only when we don't need him?

You see, Lord, you have me very annoyed here. First you tell me I shouldn't pursue the power of the world but should serve you. Then, when serving you puts me out on a limb with nowhere to go, you tell me I shouldn't put you to the test. You are driving me crazy with this. I didn't want to be stuck there in the first place, and you expect to take your sweet time doing whatever else you have to do while I wait, afraid out of my wits, and eventually fall off. My faith is not that strong that I can take this easily.

Bless my mind to illuminate me with your wisdom;
bless my lips to allow me to speak your word;
and bless my heart that I might live the gospel.

1

Foundations of the Just War

Prologue

I am not sure what started the animosity between Christopher O'Brien and me. We didn't live near each other and had little to do with each other outside of school. In fact, we didn't have all that much to do with each other in school. But whatever the origin, we didn't like each other.

This mutual dislike soon expressed itself whenever we were near. In one class during our elementary school years, I sat in front of him. Christopher inserted a straight pin into his pencil eraser and proceeded to tap on my back with the point, leaving little dots of red on my shirt. I would trip him whenever he would return to his desk from doing sums on the blackboard. We knew that the sisters who taught us were angry at our activities, so it didn't take us long to figure out quieter ways to torment each other.

It isn't easy to maintain subtle antagonism for long when you are twelve. One afternoon during recess Christopher hit me in the back of the head with a snowball containing a stone. At least I was fairly sure it was Christopher. So I pushed him and he pushed me back, and before either of us knew it we were rolling around on the snowy parking lot that was our playground during school. Of course, we attracted a circle of kids who were cheering on the fight, and of course, that circle of cheering kids attracted the attention of the nun on duty who promptly brought us to our feet and to our homeroom teacher, Sister Ricardus.

Sister Ricardus was an unnaturally good-humored nun, considering that she had to deal with forty preadolescents every day of the week, and considering the name she carried. We were nervous, though, because we knew she was near her limit. She just smiled at us and sent us off to see Father Meagher.

We walked to the rectory, but not too quickly. Father Meagher was a large man with a face like raw meat, and neither of us was eager to find out what he would say. The rectory was dark; it was always dark, and it smelled vaguely of cheap cigars. We followed a barked command into The Office.

Father Meagher sat behind a large desk in the large room, his hands folded across his stomach like some version of Sidney Greenstreet. After looking at us stand there, shifting from foot to foot for a while, he coughed that this nonsense was going to end today.

He stood up and walked out of The Office. We followed. Into the Parish Hall. The linoleum was going to be waxed that day, so all the chairs had been piled up on one side. We stood in the middle of the cleared floor.

"Since you gentlemen apparently have a problem, I suggest you settle it here and now." I had no idea what he meant, so I looked at him dumbly.

"Come on, you two. I don't have all afternoon. Get to it." Christopher understood before I did, so he balled up his fists and held them out before him, ready to fight.

I had never been in a fistfight before and wasn't too keen on the idea, but it was obvious that Father Meagher's intention was that we would get it all "out of our system," have a decent bloodletting, and establish dominance of one of us once and for all.

So I made my fists and began circling Christopher, waiting for him to initiate the fight, hoping that he had a better idea about how to start this thing than I had.

He did.

I don't know why, exactly, but I couldn't hit Christopher hard in the face. I popped him decently in the stomach now and then, but when it came time to hit him anywhere near his head, I couldn't. For some reason I kept pulling my punches there; perhaps I was afraid I was going to hurt him. In any event, he had no such scruple. I was soon bleeding from my nose and mouth.

I have no idea how long we fought, only that the front of my shirt was a mess. Finally, Father Meagher broke it up with a terse "That's it." I dropped my arms and watched Christopher bounce around like some early version of Sugar Ray Leonard. He put an arm around my shoulder and gave me a toothy grin in a show of magnanimity that only victors can afford. Father Meagher was smiling also. He looked at us both— Christopher pink-faced, barely sweating; me, dripping on the linoleum. He told Christopher to get going while he helped me clean up.

I don't remember walking into the men's room, but I do recall the sink and the small, metal case of Red Cross first aid supplies Father Meagher produced from somewhere. He washed my face, put pieces of cotton balls up my nostrils to stop the bleeding and was painting the cuts with Mercurochrome that burned as bad as it looked. As he worked on my lower lip, this priest who was now my cornerman spoke quietly to me.

"Your eyes will get black. On you it will be an improvement. Look, I've only got two words of advice for you. When you are in a fight, keep your mouth closed. And always remember, you don't have to hate him; you just have to hit him."

When I got home, I told my parents I had fallen down some stairs. My father knew I had lost.

—⁓—

■ Sometimes before we can go forward we need to go back and look at history. The question that occurs to me is how the church arrived at the position that some wars can be considered not only justifiable but also consistent with the demands of the gospel. In this chapter I will examine the basic formulation of just war theory as it occurred in the history of Christian thought. As we shall see in subsequent chapters, the Christian concerns about justifying warfare set the tone for subsequent secular justifications.

It is generally conceded that the wellspring of just war theory lies in St. Augustine of Hippo's *City of God,* a monument of philosophical theology begun in 413 CE and completed in 426. As background to *City of God* it is important to bear in mind that apparently the early Christian church, from the end of the New Testament period until about 170, was generally pacifistic. As Roland Bainton points out (66–69), there is no record of any Christian writer approving of Christian participation in warfare until the time of the emperor Constantine, circa 330, and no evidence of Christians serving in the army of the Roman Empire until 173. Much of the New Testament scholarship that has been published over the past twenty years supports Bainton's conclusion, and from scholars who represent a variety of theological perspectives. In *Jesus and the Victory of God,* Anglican evangelical N. T. Wright gives strong indications of Jesus's pacifism through, among other things, his rejection of the Zealot's program; and liberal theologian Marcus Borg has written, "One of the most certain results of historical scholarship is that Jesus and the early Christian movement of the first three centuries practiced non-violence. One of the most encouraging developments of our time is that an increasing number of Christians are willing to take seriously the non-violent stance of Jesus and early Christianity" (Borg 2005).

But even our own examination of early church writings indicates how some of the followers of Christ displayed their attitude toward war. By the time Tertullian, a father of the church, writes *De Corona* in 204, we see him condemning the voluntary enlistment of Christians in the Roman army, which also, interestingly, served as a domestic police force for the empire. Tertullian frames his objections in a series of rhetorical questions:

> I think we must first inquire whether warfare is proper at all for Christians. . . . Do we believe it lawful for a human oath [of military allegiance] to be superadded to one divine, for man to come under promise to another master after Christ, and to abjure father, mother, and all nearest relatives, whom even the law has commanded us to honor and love next to God Himself . . . ? Should it be held lawful to make an occupation of the sword when the Lord proclaims that he who uses the sword shall perish by the sword? And shall the son of peace take part in battle when it does not even become him to sue at the law courts? And shall he apply the chain, and the prison, and the torture, and the punishment who is not the avenger even of his own wrongs? . . . Shall he keep guard before the temples which he has renounced? . . . And shall he diligently protect by night those who in daytime he has put to flight by his exorcisms, leaning and resting on the spear with which Christ's side was pierced? Shall he carry a flag, too, hostile to Christ? . . . You may see by a slight survey how many other offences are involved in the performance of military officers which we must hold to involve a trans-

gression of God's law. The very carrying over of the name from the camp of light to the camp of darkness is a violation of it. (*De Corona* IX)

The basis of Tertullian's objection to Christian involvement with the military should be obvious to anyone with even a cursory knowledge of the gospel. We will return to analyze this more fully below, since I take his argument to be paradigmatic—not only as a description of the attitude of the early church toward the military, but also as the best summary of the negative argument for Christian pacifism. As we shall see, Tertullian's argument contains the seeds of rebuttal to some of the major points raised by St. Augustine.

Tertullian's *De Corona* was written during the time when the Christian community was a minority in the Roman Empire and undergoing sporadic persecution by the state. With the accession of Constantine to the throne of Rome, Christianity was brought into comity with the empire, and Constantine himself was baptized on his deathbed in 337. This event in particular bestowed what would be the final and most important imprimatur on the acceptability of the church to the empire, as well as the acceptability of the empire to the church. By the time we reach 380, the emperor Gratian decreed that Christianity was the official religion of the empire in the Edict of Thessalonica, accepted the teachings of the Council of Nicaea of 379, and rejected the title and honorifics associated with the position of Pontifex Maximus in 383. In less than fifty years, the relation between church and empire underwent an enormous change with considerable implications for both institutions.

Thus, when Augustine begins writing *City of God* in 413, he is addressing a church that has been substantially assimilated into the empire. What this practice of assimilation needed, however, was a secure theological and philosophical foundation. Not only would the Christians who followed the pacifistic ways of the early church need to be instructed on their duties and obligations, but also Augustine realized that he would have to answer pagan criticisms of Christianity. By this point in the history of the empire, Rome had suffered repeated assaults by the barbarians, many of whom (to make it worse) were adherents of Arianism. A fair number of pagan Roman authors were blaming the rise of Christianity for the sorry state of Roman defenses, because a state religion that, in its sacred texts, appears to reject violence in favor of a command to love would necessarily undermine the empire's martial spirit as well as its capacity to defend itself against alien invaders. In order to accomplish the twofold end of instructing Christians and answering critics, Augustine followed the lead of his teacher, St. Ambrose, and utilized sources from the pagan philosophers such as Cicero as well as the Old Testament to formulate his argument.

Nonetheless, the primary problem facing Augustine is precisely the reconciliation of Christian participation in warfare with Christ's teachings in the gospel. In other words, how is Augustine able to answer the objections of Tertullian, who argues that even the military's police function is antithetical to Christian life and practice? In *Contra Faustum* Augustine begins his answer, analyzing why war has been considered wrong:

> What is the evil in war? Is it the death of some who will soon die in any case, that others may live in peaceful subjection? This is mere cowardly dislike, not any religious feeling. The real evils in war are love of violence, revengeful cruelty, fierce and implacable enmity, wild resistance and the lust of power and such like; and it is generally to punish these things, when force is required to inflict the punishment, that, in obedience to God or some lawful authority, good men undertake wars, when they find themselves in such a position as regards the conduct of human affairs, that right conduct requires them to act or to make others act in this way. (*Contra Faustum*, 22, 74)

What Augustine is doing in this passage is very interesting and presages his strategy brought to fruition in *City of God*. I think that it is clear that Augustine is attempting to distinguish the violent *actions* that soldiers perform in the conduct of a war or military campaign from the *spiritual* constitution and disposition of their souls. By positing a dichotomy between outward, physical actions and interior, spiritual motivations or affects, Augustine locates the sinfulness of warfare not in the killing of others but in the willful love of violence, cruelty, and so forth. Later in this same work, Augustine makes his position even more explicit:

> If it is supposed that God could not enjoin warfare, because in after times it was said by the Lord Jesus Christ, "I say to you that you should not resist evil, but if anyone strikes you on the right cheek, then also turn to him the left," the answer is that what is here required is not a bodily action but an inward disposition. The sacred seat of virtue is the heart, and such were the hearts of our fathers, the righteous men of old. But order required such a regulation of events, and such a distinction of times, such as to show first of all that even earthly blessings (for so temporal kingdoms and victory over enemies are considered to be . . .) are entirely under the control and at the disposal of the one true God. (*Contra Faustum*, 22, 76)

After evoking and elucidating upon Romans 13, Augustine has the basic structure of a Christian-based just war theory in place:

1. The act of killing is, in itself, not evil, since all persons eventually will die anyway.
2. What is determinative of the moral status of war lies not in its outward aspects but within the interior disposition of those who wage it.
3. Since the temporal order and civil authority are ordained by God and controlled by him [derived from Augustine's understanding of Romans 13], we are required to obey rightful authority: to obey rightful authority is, ultimately, to show obedience to God himself.

It would clearly be absurd to argue that Augustine's intention is to sanction whatever the civil authority commands without further reflection. Blind obedience is as odious to him as absolute pacifism. So, in this following text Augustine provides a rudimentary analysis of the kinds of wars Christians ought to engage in:

A great deal depends upon the causes for which men undertake wars, and on the authority they have for doing so; for the natural order which seeks the peace of mankind ordains that the monarch should have the power of undertaking war if he thinks it advisable, and that the soldiers should perform their military duties on behalf of the peace and safety of the community. When war is undertaken in obedience to God, who would rebuke or humble or crush the pride of man, it must be allowed to be a righteous war. . . . (*Contra Faustum*, 22, 75)

In this passage Augustine anticipates the theory of natural law that will, eight centuries in the future, be completely enunciated by St. Thomas Aquinas. God has so structured the universe that it is obvious, even to those who do not have the benefit of divine revelation, that his will is that mankind live in peace and order. This is ultimately why God ordains that the civil authorities should be obeyed, even in those situations where they are not Christian authorities: the state's authority over its citizens is justified if the state maintains peace—it is acting according to the will of God insofar as it allows its citizens to flourish. If any other nation or people violates this peace and threatens the safety of the citizens, that other nation is violating God's will. And since God would rebuke, humble, and crush this prideful nation, we, who are God's instruments on earth through the authority of the state, must engage in warfare in order to restore God's order and do his will.

With this as a background, then, we can now turn to the *City of God* for the most complete enunciation of just war theory that Augustine provides.

> After the state or city comes the world, the third circle of human society—the first being the house, the second the city. And the world, as it is larger, so is it more full of dangers. . . . And here, in the first place, man is separated from man by the difference of language. . . . For their common nature is no help to friendliness when they are prevented by diversity of language from conveying their sentiments to one another. . . . But the imperial city has endeavored to impose on subject nations not only her yoke, but her language, as a bond of peace. . . . This is true; but how many great wars, how much slaughter and bloodshed, have provided this unity! And though these are past, the end of these miseries is not yet come. . . . But, say they, the wise men will wage just wars. As if he would not all the rather lament the necessity of just wars, if he remembers that he is a man; for if they were not just he would not wage them, and would, therefore, be delivered from all wars. For it is in the wrongdoing of the opposing party which compels the wise man to wage just wars; and this wrong-doing, even though it give rise to no war, would still be a matter of grief to man because it is man's wrong-doing. Let everyone, then, who thinks with pain on all these great evils, so horrible, so ruthless, acknowledge that this is a misery. And if one either endure or think of this without mental pain, this is a more miserable plight still, for he thinks himself happy because he has lost human feeling. (*City of God*, 19, 7)

Since this passage is so important for the subsequent development and elaboration of just war theory, I would like to spend a little bit of time explaining what Augustine accomplishes (or attempts to accomplish) within it. It is clear that Augustine means to imply in the very first sentence that states are part of the natural order—an expansion, if you will, of the fundamental unit of human society. It is important to note that Augustine believed, along with the prevailing thought of his time, that humans could reach the fullest development of their personhood only within communal relations: first and foremost the family, from which we derive our lives and our upbringing, and secondly the state (the "city"), from which we derive our identity, become fully formed, and pursue the good in common with others.

Augustine sees this second aspect as so important, in fact, that he later on (19, 24) maintains that a people or nation is defined as "an assemblage of reasonable beings bound together by a common agreement as to the objects of their love; thus in order to discover the character of any people, we have only to observe what they love." It is this notion of *loving* in common that binds a nation together. Insofar as the nation is rational and therefore able to apprehend the good and, ultimately, discover God's hand behind the operation of the cosmos, to that extent is the nation, and the citizens who comprise it, reaching its fulfillment. Thus, one nation may well be superior to another if the object of the former's love is better than the latter's.

Augustine's endorsement of civil society is not unqualified, however. He does argue (19, 24) that states which are ungodly (i.e., which have not yet accepted the faith) are void of true justice, and that a people who are alienated from God are miserable. Even with this qualification in mind, though, Augustine continues to maintain that it is in the interest of the church to enjoy the peace that even a pagan state provides (19, 26). Though the peace that arises from a pagan state is not even remotely comparable to the fullness of peace that Christians enjoy, ". . . what is perverted must of necessity be in harmony with, and in dependence on, and in some part of the order of things, for otherwise it would have no existence at all" (19, 12). In short, even the peace of the pagan state is related to and dependent upon the peace God gives his people and is, therefore, something that should be pursued and maintained.

By placing the state in such a primary relation to persons, Augustine is able to make the case that one of the most important functions of the state, if not its most important overall, is to foster peace and security for its citizens, especially considering the enormous threats posed by the world external to the state.

One of the things I find most interesting in this passage is Augustine's location of at least part of the problem of external threats to differences in language. He anticipates the work of some twentieth-century political philosophers—most notably Jürgen Habermas—by implying that many of the difficulties we face with one another arise from difficulty in establishing communication. In addition, and much more significantly, Augustine here provides an endorsement—albeit a strongly qualified one—for the expansion of the Roman Empire. On this reading, one of the great gifts that the empire had bestowed on humanity was the unity it achieved among many and diverse subjected peoples and nations. By conquering the neighboring nations, making them Latin speakers and ultimately part of the empire through assimilation, the empire managed to expand its community so that more and more nations could become involved together in the pursuit of the good in an atmosphere of peace and security. But clearly, Augustine qualifies, this unity which is a good thing has been achieved at a very great price: the cost of war and bloodshed. Even though the empire has achieved a good result, Augustine avers that we must not forget that the means it used to achieve it were miserable, so much so that no wise person would pursue such a course unless it were necessary.

It is interesting, though not particularly surprising, that Augustine stops his review of history at this point, for if he were to continue on with his reflections on the foundation of the empire, I think he would be forced to conclude that the imperial expansionism that Rome engaged in was neither wise nor in keeping with what I will anachronistically call his natural law theory. Since the established order of nations is one ordained by God for the purpose of furthering peace and security, and since just wars—which are the will of God—are always defensive and necessary, Roman imperial expansion was contrary to God's will and in violation of the natural law governing the universe. I am not sure what conclusion Augustine would have reached if he had followed this line of reasoning, but it certainly seems that the genealogy of "legitimate civil authority ordained by God" could be called into question by the very argument Augustine uses to sustain it. It would seem that once the civil authority has been extended illegitimately, all exercise of authority within that sphere would also be illegitimate and corrupt. The child of the thief does not gain legitimate title to the stolen goods simply through the laws of inheritance; justice would demand the restoration of the status quo ante.

Notwithstanding this line of objection, Augustine accepts the then current extension of the Roman Empire as a given. What the world outside the empire's borders contains are threats as well as invading nations intent on doing harm and performing actions contrary to the will of God. It is this type of wrongdoing that makes war necessary. War is not to be entered into lightly or without significant reason. Clearly, Augustine means justified warfare to be a last resort, when entreaty and negotiation—the fruits of communication—have been exhausted and the wrongdoing of the attacker "compels" the wise to fight and kill.

War is a terrible enterprise and brings with it much misery. But Augustine avers at the end of the passage that an attitude of peace at any price is even worse. It is important to stress Augustine's emphasis on the point that war is justifiable only if it is *necessary:* if the state, utilizing all of its wisdom, finds itself *compelled* to fight the encroachments of the enemy through force of arms. War is so bad that it should be entered into only in extreme circumstances, when there are no other alternatives that would preserve the integrity and function of the state under attack. But, at the same time and even understanding how miserable and anguishing war is, it would be even more miserable to suffer the wrongdoings of the attacker. When faced with evil alternatives, prudence would dictate that the lesser evil ought to be pursued.

Augustine does something very interesting in the last long passage I quoted from above (19, 7). Throughout most of his discussion of war and the role of civil society, Augustine refers to "the state" or "the nation" or "the earthly city." But midway through this chapter, he unaccountably shifts and says, "But they say the wise *man* will wage just wars" (emphasis added). He changes his analysis from focusing on the corporate act of a state deciding to wage war to that of an individual deciding to wage war. Why does he do this?

I do not think Augustine is talking about individual citizens or even individual Christian citizens in this context. Much of what I take to be his theory relies upon the individual Christian's duty to obey the legitimate civil authority when it decides that war is justified. It is possible that by "wise man" Augustine is referring to the emperor, who will ultimately make the decision whether it is necessary to go to war or not. I tend to reject this interpretation because I think Augustine could have easily referred to the "wise ruler" or "wise emperor" if that were his intention. Rather, I think it is more plausible to assume that Augustine is analogizing the state to an individual in order to bring out a key feature of his theory.

Earlier in this chapter I discussed what I took to be Augustine's initial response to Tertullian's position as representative of a pacifistic church. In that response, Augustine argues that the real evil of war lies in the internal disposition of persons; thus, Christians may engage in warfare if they are acting out of obedience to God's will and without the *love* of violence or cruelty that accompanies warfare. I believe that in this passage Augustine is making the same point analogically with regard to the state's motivations. Just as an individual Christian may engage in battle if his heart is pure and his dispositions are rightly ordered to God's will, so may a state engage in conducting a war if it does so with the right disposition. Therefore, a key element in a war's being just is that the state is not engaging in it for the greed that underlies expansionism or conquest, or for the love of violence, or for making itself more powerful, or for revenge. More positively expressed, states may engage in war in order to do God's will, namely, to preserve the peace and security of the natural order ordained by God when all peaceful alternatives have failed.

It remains, then, to give at least a cursory evaluation of the position Augustine has outlined as compared to Tertullian before proceeding to the next chapter. Augustine is a saint, a father of the church, a good theologian, and a wonderful philosopher. He is also wrong.

The fundamental mistake Augustine makes occurs very early in my discussion of his position. When Augustine argues that it is the internal disposition of the soldier that makes warfare either right or wrong, he introduces a division in our conception of persons and what it means to be a disciple of Christ that plagues the church to the present. To argue that the church is concerned with our souls while the state is concerned with our bodies—and this is the point behind Augustine's image of the two cities—is to introduce a dichotomy that yields all sorts of dilemmas and ultimately leads us further from the Lord. This view can be used to sanction the participation of Christians not only in warfare but in other forms of violence as well, from recognizing the legitimacy of abortion to the exploitation of workers and eventually the commodification of all God's children. What matters, on Augustine's view, is the Christian's internal disposition: all is permissible if only we are disposed the right way.

The fundamental differences between Augustine and Christian just war theorists on the one hand, and Tertullian and Christian pacifists on the other is precisely, first, that Tertullian's viewpoint does not admit of the distinction the way Augustine frames it, and second, Tertullian interprets Jesus's injunction against violence and for peacemaking in a more literal and concrete way.

Examining the extended excerpt from *De Corona* with which I began this chapter, it is clear that Tertullian is quite focused on the internal dispositions of Christians. His first rhetorical question is whether it is proper to swear an allegiance to the state, to attempt to serve another master in addition to Christ. Clearly, Tertullian believes that our disposition to follow Christ entails not only the transformation of our hearts and souls but also the comportment of our bodies. Tertullian's view is that the call to follow Christ is more totalizing than Augustine seems to admit. The commandment to love one another is not simply a call to develop and maintain a particular interior disposition. It is also a call that commands as well as forbids certain actions in themselves, because there is no way that performing those acts can be consistent with the call.

Let me hasten to add at this point that Augustine is not completely wrong. Similar actions can really be very different depending on the internal dispositions of the actors. For example, both a mugger and a surgeon use a knife to cut the flesh of others, but since the surgeon is cutting to help the

30

patient and the mugger is acting out of anger or disregard for his victim, we can distinguish the two accordingly. What an action is depends greatly upon the motivation of the person acting. But what Augustine glosses over is that class of actions that are wrong *simpliciter*, regardless of the actor's motives. Adultery, for example, would be one of these. Even if each of the participants in the adulterous relationship intended their sexual liaison to be only an expression of the love they have for each other, it is still adulterous and sinful: their marital vows preclude such actions even if their internal dispositions are pure. I think it is simply so clear that the gospel includes violence and killing on the list of actions that Christians may not perform that I honestly do not know what more could be added.

Augustine's interpretation of Matthew 5:39 is a case in point. To argue as Augustine does that the verse, "But this I say to you: offer no resistance to the wicked. On the contrary, if anyone hits you on the right cheek, offer him the other as well" is not to be taken at all literally but only pertains to an inward disposition is just plain foolish. It is clear that Jesus is talking about actions that must flow from a heart that is obedient to the Word. There is no way I can read the passage and consider that Jesus meant to teach us: "Form a deep abiding love for the one who strikes you, and then knock his teeth out in response to his aggression."

Rather, what Jesus is doing in this passage precisely undercuts Augustine's fundamental argument. Jesus is recounting and examining a principle that seems to be within us naturally and which is expressed in Exodus 21. That text, and the ones surrounding it, explain the conditions under which violent responses to violence are permissible, and those responses are vested in the legitimate authority of the nation. The *judges* of the offense are instructed to award "life for life, eye for eye, tooth for tooth, hand for hand." This is the law Yahweh gave to his people, and it serves as a compendium of required punishments and retributions to be meted out by the nation against evildoers: harming someone is wrong, but harming with the disposition to punish or seeking retribution is both right and required. When Jesus overturns these mandatory sentencing guidelines, he is clearly indicating that what stood before as justifications no longer stand. The internal disposition that the law recognized as making the violence against the evildoer permissible is no longer valid. There is, therefore, no internal disposition that transforms violent responses to violence into permissible ones. Violence is not an option for Christians.

Nor is this enough.

Nonviolence is insufficient as a response to evildoers. Just ten verses before this injunction, Jesus says, "But I say this to you, if a man looks at a woman lustfully, he has already committed adultery with her in his heart" (Matt. 5:28). Jesus makes it plain that merely refraining from performing a wrong action is not enough to avoid sin. Augustine was right to stress the development of internal dispositions; he just emphasized it in the wrong way. Of course we should not behave violently, even in response to wrongful violence done to us. But we should also not even have the desire to be violent. The internal disposition that we must develop and cultivate in order to follow Jesus and avoid sin is the disposition to love. "But I say this to you, love your enemies and pray for those who persecute you" (Matt. 5:44).

Augustine mistakenly reverses the process. If we are transformed and have our natural predispositions changed from lust and desire for violence to a disposition to love, our actions will flow from that. Jesus does not need to give an explicit prohibition against warfare or killing or violence. To do that would be to stress the negative, the refraining from prohibited actions. If we are formed by him, such prohibitions are unnecessary, because it would not occur to us to do otherwise. And if it did occur to us, we would recognize such actions as separating us from him.

Tertullian amplifies this point in *De Corona* XI. He shows little patience with the kind of argument that Augustine raises that states that war is justifiable only if, among other things, the state is compelled to fight the enemy, that is, if war is a response of practical necessity. As if in response to that point, Tertullian writes

> A state of faith admits no plea of necessity. They are under no necessity to sin ... because there is a higher necessity to dread denying and to undergo martyrdom than to escape from suffering and to render the homage required. (*De Corona* XI)

Tertullian here attacks the notion of compelled necessity to wage war and maintains that faithfulness to the Word is of a higher necessity, even if that would result in suffering and death. The idea of a just war as necessary is one that underlies much contemporary analysis and deserves to be treated in its own chapter.

Second Meditation

1 Samuel 8:4–9

The elders of Israel all assembled, went back to Samuel at Ramah, and said, "Look, you are old, and your sons are not following your example. So give us a king to judge us, like the other nations."

Samuel thought that it was wrong of them to say, "Let us have a king to judge us," so he prayed to Yahweh. But Yahweh said to Samuel, "Obey the voice of the people in all that they say to you: it is not you they have rejected but me, not wishing me to reign over them any more. They are now doing to you exactly what they have done to me since the day I brought them out of Egypt until now, deserting me and serving other gods. So, do what they ask; only, you must give them a solemn warning, and must tell them what the king who is to reign over them will do."

■ Lord, help me remember I am always in your presence.

Lord, you strike me as being unreasonable here. Samuel is old and appointed his sons judges, but they are corrupt—taking bribes and letting their judgments go to the highest bidders. This is not good, so of course the elders are annoyed. Why not just fix the problem instead of allowing it to get out of hand in the first place?

And I have to admit that I don't see this episode as that big of a deal. I can't tell what the differences are in this case between a judge, a king, a prime minister, or a president. In each case there's an intermediary between you and your people who tells them what they should do. And you are just as capable of working through any one of them as through any other. Or not, considering what you allowed Samuel's sons to get away with. So the form of governance can't be the point of this passage.

I am coming up with two other issues, then, that are related to each other. As I ponder this I see that you are looking into the heart of your people and know that their request for a king has nothing to do with the graft of Samuel's sons. Their corruption is just a convenient excuse your people are using to justify their request. As you say, they are rejecting you. They do not wish to live under your guidance. And why is that? Here is the other issue: they want to be just like all the other nations. Perhaps there is a notion of embarrassment they have; maybe Israel thinks that she looks rather primitive or backward when she compares herself to the rest of the world, so she desires to join more fully into the community of nations by having a government that is more congruent with or understandable to her neighbors. Perhaps that was what St. Augustine was trying to achieve with his work, some of which I spoke of in the last chapter: perhaps he felt that the church needed to be like other groups in the empire and was trying to work out a compromise by splitting your city in half in some ways—a Solomonic response to the pressure we feel to be like others. And maybe that trend has continued with your church to the present as we tend to see the problems of the world through the lenses of states and state power and consider ourselves "just like" other citizens. We do not want to be apart or different or follow paths that we might have to justify to those whose affection or respect we desire. And in the next chapter I think we will see what effect this has.

I remember using the same kind of argument with my mother. I wanted to do something or another, and I used the example of "all my friends are doing it." Her reply was something like, "If all your friends wanted to jump off the Brooklyn Bridge, would you go, too?" I recall that the first time she said this to me, I answered "yes," figuring that since there would be no one to play with, I might as well jump also. She hit me in the back of the head with a wooden spoon, which, I take it, was the standard reaction of Italian mothers to stupid remarks by sons.

Separated from that incident by more than forty years, and having sons of my own, I recognize the appropriate use of spoons for such a purpose. There are some things that simply are too stupid for reasoned discourse, and a loving dope-slap works a bit better than rational retorts.

But you don't slap Israel with a spoon or whatever divine equivalent you happen to have at hand. You consent. Of course, following this passage you detail the trouble Israel will have with a king: conscription of their young men into the army, taxation, and ultimately the slavery your people will endure at the hands of their ruler. You knew that they wouldn't listen to the reasoning, that they were so concerned with being like all the other nations that they would demand a king to replace you.

That seems like such a foolish thing for your people to want. I don't really know why Israel wants to be like other nations when it is so clearly *not* like them. The Israelites have a relationship with you that no other people has, and it's very clear that this relationship is the one that you yourself prefer. You do not want your people to bow to kings or prime ministers or presidents, nor do you want us to do homage to any person or thing or institution but you. You see no good coming from it, and still you allow it to happen.

I am not sure what is so different about this time in the life of your people Israel. You point out that your people had rejected you constantly since you brought them out of Egypt, and with this event you decide that it is time to go along with it. Sounds to me as though you are disgusted with all the nonsense; so, finally, at the end of your patience, you let your people go. You will not be stiff-necked like the pharaoh and allow pride to get in the way. But even so, you do sound more than a little miffed.

What good could come from rejecting you? Now your people are just like everyone else, and I can't imagine that as a good thing. I do understand the lack of faith at the root of their rejection. We don't see you clearly enough so we think we are really left to our own devices. We know that you are there, somewhere; but if we want anything done, and done in a timely manner and in a way that we can understand, we figure that we ought to do it ourselves. You have given me a mind to think with and hands to work with, so that must mean that you want me to rely on myself. And I come to rely on myself so much that I no longer think to rely on you.

Is that it? You have brought me to reflect first on Israel then to bring me to your people now, and from all of your people now down to myself. Now I am at the point where I can see myself relying on my own power and will. Not needing you, I find myself separating myself from you. But wait a moment: you did give me a mind, and you did give me hands, and I know I am supposed to use them, and I am just not sure how I am to do that and still rely upon you. So many things look like they are up to me to change them, and I know also that you do not want me standing around like I'm waiting for a bus. I know you want me to do something, all the while trusting that you are there and still in control. But like Israel, I see the graft and corruption where I expected to see your hand, and I feel lost. I know in my head that I am rationalizing, just like Israel, trying to justify my own pride, but many times I feel as though you are too busy or are testing me or are doing something else I don't understand. So I end up behaving like the pagans and rely more and more on myself.

Bless my mind to illuminate me with your wisdom;
bless my lips to allow me to speak your word;
and bless my heart that I might live the gospel.

2

The Just War in Contemporary Thought

Prologue

It has often been said that no one hates wars more than the soldiers who fight in them. I have always believed this. Who could better understand the horror, death, and destruction than those tasked with performing them as well as suffering them?

Yet I am not so sure that the hatred of war that soldiers feel is completely unalloyed. It seems a bit more mixed with something else— perhaps admiration or affection. And if it is true that soldiers consider war with some felicitous feelings, I have to wonder how much the rest of us who have not experienced it may love it even as we fear and hate it. I am not thinking here of the camaraderie or close feelings of kinship that soldiers report having with one another. This is a unity brought about through facing a common danger and is something that many of us may have felt in less exacting circumstances. Rather, there seems to be something about this ultimate struggle between large groups of trained troops that excites a marveling pleasure in all of us, not at all unlike the marveling pleasure some feel at watching boxing matches. It is a spectacular brutality, and we cheer even as we wince.

I was led to this reflection by considering the Battle of Fredericksburg, mid-December of 1862. At that time, a significant portion of the Confederate forces were entrenched at Marye's Heights outside the city of Fredericksburg. In order to break the line of the Confederate army, the Union commander, General Burnside, ordered that Marye's Heights be taken. Wave after wave of Union troops stormed the Confederate position throughout the day of December 13, and each was repulsed with enormous losses: over 8,000 Union soldiers were killed or wounded in this one assault during this one day in the war.

In the middle of what must have been a ghastly carnage, the Confederate commander, General Robert E. Lee, turned to his subordinate General Longstreet and said, "It is well that war is so terrible. We should grow too fond of it."

I think I understand the terribleness a bit better than I do the fondness, for Lee was only worried about growing too fond of it. Perhaps the fondness that Lee felt had something to do with the victory he was sure to win, especially with such relatively few casualties to his own troops. Perhaps he felt a particular exhilaration at being able to impose his will upon his enemy.

Yet I wonder if there isn't also a fondness for war even in defeat. We seem to admire Napoleon's losses as much as his victories—witness the descriptions of his Imperial Guard at Waterloo—and we appreciate the achievements of Rommel and Lee in their losing efforts as well as their victorious ones, and we can also consider Texans and the Alamo and how they take that defeat as in some way defining. Sometimes it seems that even as we use military metaphors to describe our sports, perhaps the reverse is also true: the way we look at and appreciate war is the way we look at and appreciate sports. We admire the game well played.

■ There are many contemporary formulations of just war theory, and sometimes it seems that there is little agreement among just war theorists regarding the particular aspects or interpretations of what their respective theories involve. While it is not feasible or even desirable for me to give a detailed analysis of just war theory in all of its permutations, there are fundamental features of the theory about which almost all proponents of just wars agree. Surprisingly, those basic features are essentially the same ones that Augustine alluded to in his writings. In fact, the consensus about these basic aspects has led to the codification of the rules and requirements developed and elaborated over the centuries of the just war tradition into sets and collections of international laws regarding warfare. For example, both the Geneva Convention and the Hague Convention employ the same basic standard as found in the theory we will examine.

Generally speaking, all just war theorists divide the theory into separate parts, each with an appropriate Latin name. The first part of the theory is referred to as *jus ad bellum*. This section of the theory is concerned with the justification of resorting to war in the first place. The second part of the theory is entitled *jus in bello,* and it examines how nations may conduct a war once it has begun. For example, the *jus in bello* part of the theory discusses what kind of strategy and tactics commanders of the military may employ in order to defeat the enemy. The third part of the theory is a relatively new development and is called *jus post bellum*. This aspect concerns itself with the proper way to end wars and focuses on the reestablishment of peace and security once the enemy has been defeated. Because it runs somewhat far afield of my concerns here, I will not address *jus post bellum*.

It is often convenient to think of *jus ad bellum* as providing a set of rules for going to war. There are six requirements, each of which must be satisfied by political communities in order to engage in justified warfare. In brief, *jus ad bellum* demands that:

1. There must be a *just cause* for resorting to violence.
2. A state must have the *right intention*. That is, a state must intend to fight the war only for the reasons established by the just cause elucidated under condition (1).
3. Only the *competent and designated authorities* of a state may declare war; subgroups (such as ethnic minorities) or individuals in a state may not declare war since they are not tasked with maintaining order.
4. War is justifiable only if it is the *last resort*. All other plausible and possible options for resolving the issue(s) of the just cause must be exhausted before warfare commences.
5. As far as possible, a state must ascertain that engaging in warfare assures a *high probability of success*. War or resistance must not be a futile endeavor.

6. The overall good to be achieved by engaging in warfare must be *proportionately greater* than the death, damage, and economic costs that are integral to warfare itself.

Once a state has satisfied all the requirements outlined by *jus ad bellum,* it must adhere to the two requirements of *jus in bello* for the actual prosecution of the war. In brief, these two conditions outline the constraints on the means a country at war may employ to reach its justified end or goal, especially since a state's justified end must include proportionality (condition 6 above). The two rules for the conduct of war, therefore, require that:

1. The force that nations employ must be *proportionate* to the specific ends or goals they are pursuing. This rule is directly related to (6) of *jus ad bellum* and can be seen as the application of that criterion to the battlefield, so to speak.
2. The armed forces of nations should *discriminate* between the innocent civilian population, which shall remain immune from direct and intentional attack, and those legitimate targets of military action, such as enemy combatants. I understand this requirement to preclude what some writers refer to as "means *mala in se*" or "means that are evil in themselves," such as civilian rape, ethnic cleansing, or the use of chemical or biological weapons, the employment of which is inherently indiscriminate.

While all of these rules for *jus ad bellum* and *jus in bello* appear to be rather straightforward and easily understandable, there are a number of difficulties that arise with them once they are considered more carefully. Although there are numerous problems and complex related issues that are discussed widely in the literature on just war, I shall examine only a few that are most pertinent to our discussion. In addition, for the next few pages I will take the argument in favor of just wars on its own, primarily secular terms. Most of the current Christian discussions of these criteria—notably the National Conference of Catholic Bishops in their pastoral letter *The Challenge of Peace* as a prime example—generally accept the contemporary secular arguments that underlie just war theory, their roots in Christian theology and philosophy notwithstanding. In what follows I will attempt to show that the conceptual moral difficulties facing the theory are large ones and potentially fatal to it. It is best, then, to begin with the first requirement of *jus ad bellum,* since so much of the subsequent theory rests on a clear understanding of it.

It is not often easy to determine when a just cause for war exists or what criteria a state may use in reaching the determination that a just cause is operative. Of course, there are clear-cut examples to which proponents can point to elaborate this requirement. In fact, the United Nations Charter Articles 2 and 51 point to aggression as a clear case and maintain that defensive wars are justifiable:

> Article 2, section 4: All Members [of the United Nations] shall refrain . . . from the threat or use of force against the territorial integrity or political independence of any state.

> Article 51: Nothing in the present Charter shall impair the inherent right of individual or collective self-defense if an armed attack occurs against a Member of the United Nations. . . .

By claiming that states have an "inherent right" of self-defense that justifies, among other things, their armed resistance to aggression, just war proponents are grounding their claim in one of two ways. On the one hand, they may be utilizing a form of the natural order argument employed by Augustine, Thomas Aquinas, and many medieval Christian thinkers. This argument asserts, as we have seen, that the formation and maintenance of states is something that is a natural occurrence (in theistic accounts, it has been ordained by God) and that states, therefore, have a rightful sovereignty over the people they rule. On the other hand, proponents may be using a more contemporary account that derives a state's right to defend its sovereignty and territorial integrity from the basic human rights that its citizens possess. On this rendering, the state's right is derived from the individuals' rights to self-defense and self-determination, which they transfer to the institution of the state through some sort of social contract.

Whether a state's inherent right to self-defense is antecedent to or derivative from the putative rights of individual citizens need not detain us at this point. The relevant factor is the recognition of the legitimacy of states for the purpose of promoting the common good of their people, namely, guaranteeing the peace and security of their respective citizens. The violation of this principle and all it entails is the ultimate basis for the notion of a just cause to go to war. Either because nature (or God) has ordained it or because the self-determination of individuals has created it, the fundamental role of the state is to maintain itself as the ultimate guarantor of the common good. From this it follows that the state is justified in taking whatever steps are necessary to maintain its status and function. This same principle when applied domestically entails that the state should utilize police powers in order to maintain tranquility among the populace; when applied to international interactions, this principle necessitates the state's armed resistance to external interference.

Just war theorists generally concede that actualized aggression—meaning a cross-border incursion, invasion, or other concrete violation of territorial integrity—is not the only example of a violation of a state's right to be left alone. If a hostile nation poses a serious, significant, and imminent threat, it would also be justifiable for the targeted state to engage in preemptive military action to eliminate or reduce the risk of invasion. Thus, in 1967, the state of Israel responded to Charles de Gaulle's objection to its preemptive attacks on its neighbors by claiming that the very facts that the Arab states had mobilized troops on Israel's borders and closed the Straits of Tiran to Israeli shipping constituted acts of aggression. To wait until the Arab armies crossed Israel's borders would be tantamount to abetting the aims of the enemy to destroy the Israeli state (see Johnson 1984, 21–22). It seems clear that certain kinds of credible threats to the security of a nation are justifiable grounds for war, especially if those threats portend the intention of the aggression to eliminate the targeted state.

It is important to note, however, that not all instances or examples of uninvited external interference in the affairs of a targeted state are unjustifiable. There may well be cases in which one state would be justified in going to war with another state because of the internal programs or policies that the latter state is engaged in. In the words of the United States Catholic Bishops, "War is permissible only to confront 'a real and certain danger,' that is, to protect innocent life, to preserve the conditions necessary for decent human existence, and to secure basic human rights" (section 86).

What follows from this is that a state may initiate hostile military action against another state that poses no direct threat to it if the latter state is seriously abusing the rights of its citizens, particularly the oppression of innocents (e.g., persecuting minorities or depriving some citizens of basic human dignity), or if the latter state stands in need of punishment for wrongdoing. In cases such as these, the targeted state's right to territorial integrity and noninterference in its internal affairs is voided, because the state is not behaving the way it ought. By not acting to promote the common good or maintain the peace and security of its citizens—by behaving in the opposite way, in fact—the evil state and its policies must be overthrown by whatever means necessary and replaced with a well-formed and well-functioning state that will satisfy its proper role and function.

Two recent examples will help concretize how these justifications for war operate in the realm of contemporaneous international relations.

The United States prosecuted the first Iraq war as a response to the Iraqi invasion of Kuwait. President George H. W. Bush and the government of the United States entered into war with Iraq precisely because Iraq violated the territorial integrity of a sovereign nation and attempted to absorb it as a province. Recognition of Kuwait's right to an independent existence and Iraq's unjustified aggression moved President Bush to form a coalition of countries to punish Iraq for its transgressions and correct the wrongs it had perpetrated, even though there was no direct or imminent threat to the territorial integrity of the United States or its coalition partners. Justice would be served by restoring order, peace, and security to that part of the world.

The second case is much more complex and controversial. The justification of the second Iraq war involved the invocation of the other elements of just cause. As the United States prepared for war, President George W. Bush and his surrogate, Secretary of State Colin Powell, tried to make the case that Iraq was in possession of weapons of mass destruction. Because the government of Iraq was apparently willing to use these alleged weapons, this constituted a threat to the security of the United States and its allies. The regime of Saddam Hussein was not cooperating sufficiently with the team of United Nations weapons inspectors and had demonstrated frequently over the course of nearly a decade its unwillingness to comply with United Nations resolutions to forgo those weapons and destroy its stockpiles.

It is interesting to note that during the international debate that followed, neither France nor Germany discounted the validity of American fears; they seemed to be as convinced as the government of the United States that Iraq was in possession of the weapons and was willing to use them. Their objection was based on the issue of the imminence of the threat Iraq posed to the world community. France and Germany argued that the program of weapons inspection should be continued in order to more accurately assess Iraq's capabilities before hostilities commenced. In short, these European powers were arguing that condition (4) was not satisfied: war is justified only as a last resort, if all other means to adjudicate differences have been exhausted. This is one reason why British Prime Minister Blair's claim—subsequently shown to be erroneous—that Iraq could launch missiles laden with chemical or biological warheads within forty-five minutes was so important. Blair's assertion spoke very clearly to the immediacy of the threat Iraq was posing to other nations and, implicitly, that invasion was a last resort.

Of course we know that, as of this writing, no weapons of mass destruction were found in Iraq. When it became apparent that the justification for war that the United States trumpeted most forcefully before the invasion was no longer tenable, the Bush administration began to emphasize another reason, that is, the defense of innocents. Bush and his representatives argued that Saddam Hussein's regime was corrupt and involved the wholesale and ongoing oppression and killing of groups such as the Shiite Muslims and the Kurds, as well as the torture and suppression of political dissidents; and, further, that the Iraqi government ruled by intimidation and violence rather than by the will of its citizens; and, finally, that the Iraqi government was characterized by a total disregard for the basic rights and human dignity of Iraqi citizens. In addition to the charge that innocents were suffering, the American administration maintained that Saddam Hussein's regime deserved punishment for its use of weapons of mass destruction on its own people. Military action and intervention against Hussein and his followers in the Baath Party were, therefore, justified, so that a just order might be reestablished, that is, so that a just and proper government could be formed to maintain the peace and security of the Iraqi people and promote the common good.

As stated by President Bush and other governmental officials, this rationale for offensive war against Iraq is substantial and appears to fully satisfy the requirements for just cause. It is important to note, however, that this justification was subject to a similar kind of objection as was the primary argument for just war cited previously—namely, that it did not satisfy the last-resort criterion. While no one would dispute, I am sure, that Saddam Hussein's regime was continually engaged in the oppression of the aforementioned groups, it might well be argued that not *all* nonviolent avenues to ameliorate this condition had been explored. Certainly the Bush administration could respond that many efforts had been put forth over the years—including both the northern and southern no-fly zones—and they were inadequate to solve the problem; future attempts would most likely be futile as well, considering the intractability of the regime. The dispute about the satisfaction of the last-resort criterion, then, would devolve into a conflict of judgments regarding the specific facts underlying this case.

One of the primary difficulties with the just war requirements should be apparent: it is not very clear when the conditions of just cause and last resort have been satisfied. It is obvious in the example of a rogue state initiating hostilities by a cross-border invasion that armed resistance would be justifiable according to the theory: at that point discussions or negotiations between the parties would appear to be superfluous at best, and at worst an aid to the invader. But as soon as just war theory adapts to accommodate and allow preemptive attacks by a threatened state, it is no longer clear either how much solid evidence is required or how much discussion or negotiation would be prudent. In fact, given the ease of development of some weapons of mass destruction, such as dirty bombs, and the possible use of relatively unsophisticated terrorist tactics, the mere expression of hostility by one state against another or even the discernment of maleficent intent may provide sufficient justification for preemptive attacks by a fearful and increasingly vulnerable nation.

Another difficulty with the just war criteria, at least to this point and taken as a whole, is that they seem able to justify almost all wars rather than to provide a means to limit the number of wars that would be considered just. Certainly at this point of the discussion, it is difficult to see how even the initiation of the most heinous example of war in the twentieth century could be called unjust without a considerable measure of dispute.

I believe a strong case can be made that Nazi Germany's initiation of World War II in the European theater—as well as the events that led up to it—satisfy the criteria for just cause as well as any other (see Holmes 172–76). Through his speeches and writings both before he was elected chancellor and after he became Fuehrer, Adolph Hitler argued that Germany was confronted by an international conspiracy that threatened his nation's security and survival. He identified a cabal of Marxists and Jews who were undermining the values Germans had maintained for centuries, were polluting the German spirit, destroying the German economy, and leading his *volk*—through their domination of the universities, arts, and media in particular—into a degeneracy that would eventually lead to the nation's corruption and collapse. The formulation of the Nuremberg Laws in the mid-1930s against the Jews as well as the suppression of the German Communist Party were justifiable uses of the state's police powers, since they were predicated upon the analysis of mortal threat to peace and security that those groups posed. The same could be said for the mass killings that took place in the camps during the war: supreme threats call for supreme responses.

Even Germany's annexation of the largely German Sudeten region of Czechoslovakia and its invasion of Poland are examples of just cause—the former achieved through threat and negotiation, and the latter by force of arms. Poland was awarded large areas of German territory following the First World War, even though the majority of people inhabiting those regions had voted in 1919 to remain part of the German state. If we are going to credit the value of self-determination of peoples with sufficient moral force to justify war on their behalf when that right is violated, then it is hard to exclude the activity of the Third Reich to achieve just that end. Further, it certainly seems more than plausible that the German invasion of France in 1940 could be termed a justified war of preemption, since France and its ally Great Britain posed an imminent threat to the territorial integrity of Germany.

My aim, of course, is not to justify Germany's initiation of the Holocaust or Word War II, nor am I trying to score rhetorical points against the Iraq wars. What I am attempting to show through this whole discussion is that the criteria set out and developed by just war theory are simply too flaccid and flexible to yield an outlawing of some of the most immoral and heinous activities of the last century. My point is not that the Nazis were justified in what they did—just the opposite—but just war theory does not provide a clear way to establish their immorality and, indeed, may well serve to justify their actions. If that is the case, then the problem clearly lies with the theory.

It does not matter that Hitler and the Nazis were wrong about an international Marxist-Jewish conspiracy against Germany and the West. They appear to have firmly believed their claims. Governments and individuals can act only upon what they believe to be the case. It provides no comfort either simply to assert that the Nazis were acting from erroneous judgments. If what they believed to be the case had happened to be true, what follows is that the oppression, the camps, and the invasions all would be, in large measure, good and just if not required. To employ another example, if the American and British intelligence estimates regarding Iraqi weapons of mass destruction were made in good faith, and if the Bush administration's decision to go to war was based in significant part upon those estimates, it would be unfair and unreasonable to maintain that the second Iraq war was unjust on the basis of that error. We all do the best we can with what we believe the case to be; to demand perfection in our predictive judgments seems to be an unrealistic standard. Germany in the 1930s was not a place of high moral integrity, and what the German people did was wrong. Just war theory is incapable of establishing that.

The last criterion for *jus ad bellum* I want to examine briefly is the requirement that a state may engage in war only if it has the *right intention*. To return once again to the example of the second Iraq war, the American administration continually stated that its goal was not to secure Iraqi oil for its own consumption; that it would not establish permanent military bases in Iraq unilaterally; and, more positively, that it desired to empower

Iraqi citizens to determine their own fate through the establishment of independence, sovereignty, and free elections. The Bush administration recognized that incorporating any other aim into the prosecution of the war would taint the justifiability of its actions. For the United States to derive from the war any economic or political benefit that was not directly and integrally related to the just cause would render the war predatory and a violation of the principle of noninterference. The intention a state displays through its words and actions is crucial in evaluating the morality of its warfare.

Although it might not be obvious at first glance, criterion (8) for *jus in bello* is very closely related to the right-intention requirement. The principle of discrimination has generated much discussion over the years in both academic and political circles, because the very nature of warfare itself—not merely war in our modern, technological era—seems to violate it right from the outset.

If it is possible to boil it down to its simplest and most fundamental element, what makes acts of aggression wrong in the first place is that innocents are made to suffer serious harms. It is obvious that a war, in order to be just, must not inflict harm or death or injury on innocent persons, or else it is no better (except, perhaps, quantitatively) than the original aggression. The problem facing those who wish to justify war is that it is impossible to conduct a war without harming some innocents. It is in the very nature of war that innocents will die (cf. Holmes 186–87).

Just war theory is wrong insofar as it makes "innocence" the key concept in the formulation of criterion (8); rather, it should be "civilian." In fact, some contemporary theorists recognize this and frame criterion (8) in terms of "noncombatant immunity." It is the presumption that civilians are by definition noncombatants, rather than their putative innocence, that should render them safe from harm, according to this rule. If innocence alone was the guiding concept behind this criterion, it is exceedingly hard to see how any war could be waged justly. At the very least, one side's armed forces are innocent of any wrongdoing if, for example, they are acting in defense of their nation against aggression. It is even possible that the armed forces of both sides in a conflict are innocent. Yet we never blame enemy soldiers for the battlefield killings of just warriors, even though it appears we should because just warriors are innocent and do not deserve to be harmed. On the other hand, we do hold both sides to account morally and legally for civilian deaths without inquiring into the innocence of the civilians. Additionally, we blame and prosecute soldiers on both sides of a conflict for the maltreatment or abuse of prisoners of war, as the aftermath of the Abu

Ghraib incidents indicates. The guilt or innocence of military prisoners of war does not change once they have been captured; what is relevant is that they cease to be combatants as soon as they are in custody. In fact, we term some instances of civilian killings and all cases of prisoner abuse as atrocities precisely because they violate this principle of discrimination. Thus, if war is to be justifiable, innocence cannot be the defining element of discrimination.

The problem is making *combatancy* the morally relevant feature of who may be killed justifiably in warfare. In the first place, such a move does not correspond to our moral judgments in other, similar circumstances. For example, if an armed criminal is intercepted by an armed police officer and gunfire is exchanged, the criminal will have committed *another* offense—that of trying to kill the police officer who is exercising his or her moral or civic duty. The fact that both the police officer and the criminal are armed—are combatants in the relevant sense—does not place them on an equal moral footing in regard to the shootout. The force exercised by the police officer is justified (incidentally, by the very same principles and reasoning that underlies just war theory), and the force exercised by the criminal is *not* justified precisely because the police officer is an innocent and the criminal is not. It seems obvious that innocence should be morally relevant to the question of who may be killed in war.

Yet not even the most retaliatory armistice agreement of the twentieth century—the Versailles Treaty—recognized that the deaths of Allied soldiers in combat was morally wrong and deserving of even corporate restitution on the part of the German state. Article 232 of the Versailles Treaty reads, in part:

> [Germany] will make compensation for all damage done to the *civilian population* of the Allied and Associated Powers and to their *property*. (emphasis added)

Presumably innocent Allied civilians are due compensation for all the physical or financial harms they incur from German aggression, but innocent Allied soldiers and their families are not. It is exceedingly odd that simply the status of being a combatant serves to nullify a soldier's right to have his unjust losses restored, while the status of being a noncombatant even preserves a civilian's property rights. What is even more curious about the Versailles Treaty is that in Annex I, Section 5, Germany was held financially liable for the pensions due to Allied military personnel, because of their forced involvement in the war! One philosopher maintains that the reason that we do not hold soldiers accountable for battlefield deaths is that "we draw a line between the war itself, for which the soldiers are not responsible, and the conduct of the war, for which they are responsible, at least within their own sphere of activity. . . . We draw [the line] by recognizing the nature of political obedience" (Walzer, 38–39). But this line of reasoning is more a description than an explanation; the question is simply why we draw the line of who may be *killed justifiably* the way we do.

Frankly, I am not sure why combatancy status is the determinant used to justify all battlefield killing of military personnel. I can come up with only two possible explanations.

The first explanation invokes the principle of self-defense: since all individuals have a right to the preservation of their lives, and since battlefield conditions are such that individuals on both sides of the conflict have their lives in jeopardy, all combatants are entitled to use deadly force to protect themselves from harm. While this approach seems to absolve all military personnel from guilt such that soldiers of an aggressor nation are held blameless for battlefield killings, it would also seem to shift our moral condemnation to the institution of war itself. If the institution of war is such that any instance of it places the lives of innocents at risk and further guarantees that a significant proportion of them will be killed or injured, then it seems impossible that any war could be justified. This explanation clearly undercuts just war theory itself.

The second explanation does not fare much better than the first. The killing of soldiers on the battlefield is not subject to moral evaluation because we should rather understand it as the elimination of the rival's means to wage war. On this account, soldiers on both sides are reduced to their military function alone so that we should consider them as mere instruments of governmental policy, much like tanks and fighter aircraft, rather than persons. This is a bizarre way to consider the issue. In the first place, it simply is not clear why being a member of the armed forces renders an individual's moral status as a person nil, so that he or she may be killed with impunity. In the second place, the dehumanization of the armed forces is repulsive. Reducing people to means or mere instruments so that they are devoid of even the most fundamental moral right—not to be killed unjustly—makes a mockery of any theory's claim to justice, especially when civilian property damage is counted as a moral cause for compensation.

As offensive as those provisions of the Versailles Treaty and the preceding discussion may be, they also point to a feature of wars in general that is in apparent contradiction to the notion of noncombatant immunity as well as to the notion of moral innocence. By holding the German nation liable to compensate the Allied Powers for the costs and damage incurred during the First World War, the treaty implies that, ultimately, the citizens of the German state bear moral responsibility as a whole for the war and its effects. There was no attempt to discriminate among German citizens who actively supported the war, those who merely complied with it, and those who were opposed. More interestingly, the notion of a state's liability for the waging of an unjust war is one that persists. The German nation paid restitution and compensation to the victims of the Holocaust and their survivors well into the 1990s. The costs of this national program were borne by many who had opposed the war (such as Willy Brandt, who went into exile in the 1930s and returned at war's end) as well as by a large number of German citizens who were not even born until after the war was over. Thus, we are faced with the curious and contradictory propositions that noncombatants must be held immune from harm during a war because of the principle of discrimination, but may be held liable after the war indiscriminately, that is, without regard to their degree of complicity or innocence.

Michael Walzer, in his famous *Just and Unjust Wars* (parts of which I will examine more closely in the next chapter), interprets the issue of reparations and liability differently than this, and his views deserve special attention. He writes:

> Reparations are surely due to the victims of aggressive war, and they can hardly be collected only from those members of the defeated state who were active supporters of the aggression. Instead, the costs are distributed through the tax system, and through the economic system generally, among all the citizens, often over a period of time extending to generations that had nothing to do with the war at all. In this sense, citizenship is a common destiny, and no one . . . can escape the effects of a bad regime, an ambitious or fanatic leadership, or an overreaching nationalism. But if men and women must accept this destiny, they can sometimes do so with good conscience, for the acceptance says nothing about their individual responsibility. The distribution of costs is not the distribution of guilt. . . . It might be better to say of loyal citizens who watch their government or army . . . doing terrible things that they should feel ashamed rather than responsible—unless they actually are responsible by virtue of their particular participation or acquiescence. (297)

In the initial part of this quotation, Walzer seems to cite practical reasons why all the citizens of a nation should share the destiny of paying reparations. Since those who were truly responsible for the war either cannot be identified, are no longer living, or do not have sufficient funds, reparations must be collected from all because the victims *deserve* reparations. This is hardly a convincing argument. Many persons may be unjustly injured by another, but we never look to a perpetrator's ability to pay as the standard for that person's liability. For example, if I am injured by the willful negligence of a destitute driver, then, even though I am entitled to and deserve restitution (reparations), if the guilty driver is unable to pay, I am simply out of luck; it would be wrong to insist that any group of bystanders who can afford it must make me whole; nor could I insist that the driver's children compensate me. The distribution of costs does indeed presume the distribution of responsibility.

As for the second part of Walzer's quote, I maintain that citizens should feel both ashamed and responsible for the acts of their state. As useful and interesting as Daniel Goldhagen's *Hitler's Willing Executioners* is, its overall thesis that the Holocaust depended upon the complicity of the German people is hardly surprising and may even be self-evident.

No nation can sustain any far-reaching policy, let alone a war, without its citizenry's participation and acquiescence. It would seem, then, that enthusiasm, cooperation, compliance, or even nonresistance on the part of the vast majority of the people of a state is necessary for any kind of ongoing policy initiative. It therefore follows that policies or programs that a nation sustains either are expressive of the self-determined will of the population or advance, to the best knowledge of all those involved, the common good as the nation understands it. All of this means, therefore, that a civilian population is implicated, to some substantial degree, as morally responsible in the evil actions and conduct of the regime. It is exceedingly difficult, then, to maintain that civilian populations should remain immune from harm because of their innocence. But even if one rejects this argument as too fanatical, rigid, or strict, the provision of noncombatant immunity is not secure.

It seems that one way or another, the ultimate ground for the sanctioned killing of soldiers on the battlefield rests upon the idea that since the military is necessary for the prosecution of the war, it therefore poses no moral problem that military personnel be killed. If this is the case, then noncombatantcy status should not convey immunity either: civilian populations are also necessary for war to be sustained and in a similar material sense. An army in the field must be maintained by the goods and services produced by a civilian population or supported by the tax levies imposed upon the citizenry at large. If it is also true, as it appears to be, that wars can be sustained only if the will of the people either supports it or remains passive in its acceptance of the situation, then it is fairly clear that one of the more efficient ways to defeat an intractable enemy is to target the civilian population of the state.

This program of total warfare does not characterize every armed conflict, but it is hardly a rare occurrence. Most famously in the ancient world,

Rome killed or enslaved the people of Carthage at the end of the Third Punic War, destroyed the city, and even sowed salt in the fields so that no crops could be grown there again—all to ensure that this rival city-state could not threaten Rome again. In the modern era, at least as early as 1864, General Sherman proclaimed his intention to "make the South howl" by marching to the sea and leaving a path of total destruction in his wake. Both the German air force and the Allied air force carpet bombed cities—and not only because they contained industries crucial to the war effort. Carpet bombing was intended to terrorize the citizens of the state and break their will to fight. There were no military targets in Coventry, Dresden, Hiroshima, or Nagasaki, yet those cities were destroyed in order to further the war aims of the contending nations.

Some will, no doubt, want to say that these instances are not justifiable; that they are examples of tacticians or governmental leaders bowing to the forces of expediency, that is, to finish a war as quickly as possible and by whatever means are at hand. In fact, they would argue, it is one of the purposes of *jus in bello* to eliminate these kinds of occurrences. Yet I believe it is very difficult to maintain this objection when the logical force of just war theory leads the other way. If the notion of innocence is of crucial importance to the theory, then all wars must be unjust, because all wars involve the intentional killing of innocents. If the notion of noncombatant immunity replaces innocence, then soldiers may be killed with impunity because they are necessary instruments of war. But then civilian populations are also instrumentally necessary for the prosecution of war, so they, in their homes, should be as legitimate a target as soldiers at the front. In fact, I believe that President Truman and others seeking to justify the atomic bombing of Hiroshima and Nagasaki came close to abrogating the principle of noncombatant immunity when they defended the bombing by claiming that several hundred thousand civilian deaths were justified since that prevented an estimated one million Allied soldiers from dying by invading the Japanese islands. In brief, they asserted the moral equivalence of soldiers and noncombatants in war.

Even though the bombings and destruction of cities and the killing of civilians follow from the logic of war, proponents of just wars insist that the killing of noncombatants is forbidden. In addition to the difficulty they face in framing a plausible argument for excluding noncombatants from justified death—Truman's argument in particular is problematic for them—just war theorists also have to contend with the fact that in wartime it is inevitable that civilians are killed. We have even developed a vocabulary for it: all of us are familiar with the expression "collateral damage."

The deaths of civilians in time of war is termed *collateral* because they are the unintended results of belligerent operations directed against military targets; *collateral* is used to mean "indirect." We need to recall that criterion (8) demands that no noncombatant be the *intentional, direct target* of military action. This criterion for *jus in bello* is taken so strongly that it is not uncommon for belligerent nations to construct military targets (such as ammunition dumps or munitions factories) near civilian installations (such as hospitals or schools) in hopes that enemy commanders will refrain from attacking them.

This strategy does not often work. In the first place, contemporary warfare has progressed to the point where "smart" bombs have been developed—explosive devices that can be launched or dropped with pinpoint accuracy, so that the risk of hitting nonmilitary, civilian targets has been greatly diminished. Errors, however, still occur, and mistaken targets or more than expected damage seems to remain an integral part of war. So, in the second place, the wording of condition (8) is very careful indeed: those in charge of military operations must not *intend* to target civilians *directly*. Indirect and unintentional killing of civilians, while not permissible, is not blameworthy.

What I have just described falls under the general heading of the principle of double effect, a category that has been in use in both moral theology and philosophical ethics at least since the time of St. Thomas Aquinas in the late thirteenth century. Derived from Augustine's development of internal dispositions, which we examined in the preceding chapter, double effect is addressed by St. Thomas:

> Nothing hinders one act from having two effects, only one of which is intended, while the other is beside this intention. Now moral acts take their species according to what is intended, and not according to what is beside the intention, since this is accidental as explained above. . . . Accordingly, the act of self-defense may have two effects, one in the saving of one's life, the other [in] the slaying of the aggressor. Therefore, this act, since one's intention is to save one's own life, is not unlawful. . . . And yet, though proceeding from a good intention, an act may be rendered unlawful if it be out of proportion to the end. Wherefore, if a man, in self-defense, use more than necessary violence, it would be unlawful. (*Summa Theologica,* II–II, ques. 64, art. 7)

This principle, like so much else I have only touched upon in this book, has generated voluminous discussion in both philosophical and theological circles. So, yet again, my remarks will of necessity be perfunctory.

When I first encountered this principle, I thought Thomas was directing his attention to the unforeseeable effects of an action. It does not seem fair or right to ascribe moral responsibility for the effects of an action that no one could have predicted, especially considering that all actions have multiple and various effects, some of which might reverberate indefinitely, like the ripples in water that follow from a dropped stone. But this is clearly not what Thomas is discussing. He is focused upon the foreseen effects of an act and attempting to justify an action that has both a good and a bad effect.

Like Augustine, Thomas is grappling with the prohibition against killing that all Christians are to obey, and, also like Augustine, Thomas locates the morality of the action in the intention of the actor. So, in this example, Thomas maintains that it is permissible for someone to intend to save her own life, act to defend herself and, as a simultaneous result, kill the aggressor. Since the killing of the aggressor was not part of the actor's intention, it arises indirectly from what she did intend and would be, therefore, justifiable even though foreseen by the actor.

This is a strange and noxious doctrine, notwithstanding its longevity. It renders null all moral absolutes and opens the door for all sorts of actions that ought to be prohibited. Neither killing nor adultery nor theft nor sacrilege nor apostasy—and that list could go on for a considerable time—are forbidden if their performance, even though foreseen, is not part of the direct intent of the actor. One could try to argue, following Thomas's example, that an act of killing is different from an act of self-defense precisely because it forms no part of the intent, even though the act of killing is entailed by the act of self-defense. But it is very difficult for me to separate the two in the way that seems to be required. If one knows what all the effects of an action are, then it seems to me that all of those effects must be part of the intent to act in that way, and to say otherwise appears to be a rationalization of the grossest sort.

Even if we can surmount that difficulty, the formulation of the principle is fatally defective. Clearly, when Thomas is talking about self-defense against an aggressor, he intends to hold that the act of aggression is unjust—obviously, Thomas does not wish to sanction a criminal's resistance to a police officer's lawful authority, for example. Thus, he is saying that it is permissible to kill another who is threatening one's life unjustly. But it is not at all clear how anyone could discern that what the aggressor is doing is unjust. Let me make this clear: if the justice or injustice of an action is determined by the direct intention of the actor, then it is not at all clear how we could ever know that the action of the aggressor is an unjust one. It is certainly possible that the threat to the victim's life is a foreseen yet unintended effect of an action the aggressor is performing for some other, valid reason that is the effect he is intending directly. If it is the case that we all should always support just actions, it is very difficult to know which of these mutually exclusive alternatives we ought to prefer: the aggressor's just action that unintentionally threatens an innocent, or the defender's just action that unintentionally kills the just and innocent aggressor. I think it is clear that Thomas is evaluating the aggressor's action solely on the basis of only one of its effects, regardless if the effect of threatening another's life unjustly were intended or not. If this analysis holds for the aggressor, then it should also hold for the defender. According to Thomas, if the defender were to directly intend to kill the aggressor, the defender would be wrong.

The final difficulty with the principle of double effect that I shall address concerns its application. As I indicated above, Thomas is at great pains to articulate a justification for self-defense against an unjust aggressor. It takes a great deal of casuistry if not intellectual gymnastics of the highest order to apply this principle to the purpose of justifying the killing of innocent noncombatants. Even the *Catechism of the Catholic Church* glosses over this major leap in reasoning. It states (#2263), "The legitimate defense of persons and societies is not an exception to the prohibition against the murder of the innocent that constitutes intentional killing" and goes on to cite the first sentence of Thomas's quotation above, presumably in support of its statement. Yet a few pages later the church clarifies its position:

> *Unintentional* killing is not morally imputable. But one is not exonerated from grave offense if, without proportionate reasons, he has acted in a way that brings about someone's death, even without the intention to do so. (#2269)

According to this, then, the unintentional killing of the innocent would appear to be morally permissible as long as the reasons one has for acting in a way such that the innocent's death arises indirectly are proportionate. In other words, unintentional killing is justifiable as long as a greater evil is avoided by so doing.

This dodges the issue about what grounds Thomas's formulation of the principle of double effect provides for the killing of innocents. Instead, this article introduces an apparently different criterion: one must weigh the proportionate moral values of the effects of one's actions. We see, then, that it is never right directly to intend the killing of another; but if the killing does arise indirectly, the good it produces must outweigh the effects of alternative actions.

The Catholic Church would never admit this as a consequentialist doctrine, that is, one that simply weighs the costs and benefits of alternative courses of action. Yet it appears to come awfully close to a position advocating that the (benefit of the) end does justify the (cost of the) means. Thus, if Truman's intention was to save the lives of one million Allied soldiers when he dropped the bomb on Hiroshima, and the effect of dropping the bomb was indeed to shorten the war considerably, then clearly there is no moral problem in the bombing. This would be the case for any instance of indirectly killing civilians when a greater good could be achieved.

This entire discussion of the principle of double effect is a stark one; indeed, it is as stark as the entire discussion of just war theory. To sum up this chapter, just war theory, as developed and defended both by church theologians and secular philosophers, is untenable. The criteria established by the theory are insufficient to outlaw even the most immoral of wars and even may well be used to justify them. It justifies the killing of innocents and other heinous acts—even if foreseen—as long as the intention of the actor is pure.

I am left with the distinct impression that the intellectual maneuvering and finely drawn distinctions that, on closer analysis, do not make very much sense are useful only after the fact, that is, after we have done what we wanted to do. I think that we desire war. We want war to be permissible without sacrificing all the values we hold most dear. As a result, we endeavor to manipulate and twist those values and moral principles to accommodate that desire rather than recognize war as the moral offense it is.

Third Meditation

Isaiah 6:1–10

In the year of King Uzziah's death, I saw the Lord seated on a high and lofty throne; his train filled the sanctuary. Above him stood seraphs, each one with six wings: two to cover its face, two to cover its feet and two for flying; and they were shouting these words to each other:

Holy, holy, holy is Yahweh Sabaoth.
His glory fills the whole earth.

The door-posts shook at the sound of their shouting, and the Temple was full of smoke. Then I said:

"Woe is me! I am lost,
for I am a man of unclean lips
and I live among a people of unclean lips,
and my eyes have seen the King, Yahweh Sabaoth."

Then one of the seraphs flew to me, holding in its hand a live coal which it had taken from the altar with a pair of tongs. With this it touched my mouth and said:

"Look, this has touched your lips,
your guilt has been removed
and your sin forgiven."

I heard the voice of the Lord saying:

"Whom shall I send? Who will go for us?"
And I said, "Here I am, send me." He said:

"Go, and say to this people,

57

'Listen and listen, but never understand!
Look and look, but never perceive!'
Make this people's heart coarse,
make their ears dull, shut their eyes tight,
or they will use their eyes to see,
use their ears to hear,
use their heart to understand,
and change their ways and be healed."

■ Lord, help me to remember I am always in your presence.

You remember, of course, the time I attended the conference in the late 1990s, and the famous theologian I was so anxious to meet and hear told the group of us that his faith in you was a great joy and comfort to him. He is such a merry gentleman. Anyway, I think everyone else in our circle echoed his sentiments until it came to me to speak. I confessed awe and shock at their statements, because joy and comfort so rarely occur to me when I pray my faith in you. So I told the assembly that my faith has some joy, but that seems most days to be buried. My faith is a greater source of fear and misery and anger at you. I know you are the God of peace and love, but your love and peace seem so far away—a promissory note—and the path you show me and tell me I should follow is not the one I want to walk. I know what you've told me and tell me still, and it doesn't seem to matter. Like your people Israel, I am stiff-necked. Not following your way scares me, and actually doing it scares me more. In this book I am just about to write about the "good" wars, and it puts me (as well as what I believe you ask us to do) to the test. And this is the passage you send me when I need some consolation, which is just another example of why I get so annoyed with you.

I've never read a lot of Isaiah, much less prayed on it, and I am only familiar with the Advent readings where Isaiah prophesied the Suffering Servant. As I pray this reading I'm beginning to understand better my avoidance of this book, especially since it provides yet another angle on my fear and misery.

I like to think that when you decide to come for a visit and call on us, you would do it the way you came to Samuel: the quiet voice in the night. There your presence as well as your voice were so gentle that little Samuel mistook them for old Eli. This whole passage seems to be the inverse of that calling: there you whispered and it was hard to pick you out of your own subtlety; here, you come in blazing with the angels yelling a cacophonous

58

roar. I have to ask you why that was necessary. You being you is frightening enough without an entry choreographed by Quentin Tarantino.

Yes, you are one angry deity, and there is no mistake about that, but when you are angry it is more than I can handle, and I don't mean that in any sentimental sense—you scare me to a point that is someplace beyond fear and beyond hiding. I know you love me and that I can never lose that love, but when I think about what you do to those you love, I am not consoled. Perhaps that's why I have come so close to thinking that you are beyond anger, that Jonathan Edwards was off the mark. I don't think you are *always* angry; I wouldn't know how to pray to a God who was always furious. But I do think you are angry sometimes, and I do wonder how demonstrative you get with that emotion.

It's hard for me to imagine you when you are angry, so much so that I think I anthropomorphize you too much. I mean, how could God have emotions, or what would those emotions look like were I to see them face to face? I want to think that your anger is not like mine, that it doesn't tend toward violent outbreaks. So I come very close to denying that you can be angry. Then I have to think of these kinds of scripture passages as mere metaphors, ascribing to you attributes you don't really have.

Yet I don't have the same problem with you loving me. You feeling love for me, for us, is as much an emotion, I guess, as anger is. We say that your love for us is so much better, deeper than how we love. It is a perfection that we can only approximate by images of parental love for children. And is your anger perfect, too? Is it so much deeper than the anger I feel, and so much stronger than the anger my father had when I would break his heart?

Because that is the kind of anger I think you are showing us here, the anger that accompanies a broken heart, or at least a heart broken so many times that it has moved beyond the paralysis of grief to the point of frustration and puzzlement. Is anger any less divine than love? It seems that the kind of anger that is both most righteous and most frightening is the anger that rages at a loved one who disappoints.

The inversion of Samuel continues. Isaiah says, "Here I am," just like Samuel, and you give him the prophet's commission, but this is very strange, because it looks like the message he is to declare to the people does the opposite of the other prophets' messages. How does this work? If Isaiah is proclaiming your word, how does that make your people's heart coarse and all the rest?

I have been puzzling over this a long time, and I don't know how to symbolize that pause on paper, in type. I have been sitting here so long that I've almost decided to drop this reading and pray another. It's just too hard to understand you calling a prophet who is to turn your people from you. I am starting to wonder now whether it was Isaiah's preaching that turned Israel away or whether the heart of Israel was already so coarse and ears so dull that hearing your word became less and less possible. Perhaps their understanding was so twisted that what they perceived was the opposite of what you meant. Then Isaiah's preaching turns Israel away because Israel had already moved its heart and soul away from you.

Now wait a minute. I thought that all I had to do was listen, pay attention to your word, but now it seems that listening to you may drive me away if I don't listen correctly, if somehow my heart and soul are not opened or prepared to hear what you are saying. This is hard for me to make concrete, maybe because the abstraction is so nebulous. I am trying to go through the preconditions for "listening in the right way" and don't quite know how to do it or even am sure when I have done it, if I have done it. I do have experiences of it going the other way, of someone I spoke with hearing what he wanted to hear even though I was saying the opposite. I remember that the more I tried to correct it, the worse our relationship grew. He believed I had changed my mind or lied when confronted with the difference, and yes, his heart grew coarser and he moved further from me the more I tried to speak the truth. He was convinced of what he had heard, even though I hadn't said it. Perhaps something similar goes on when we confront the terrible evils I am about to talk about. I want to kill the evil ones, and I am tempted to hear you say that it is right and just for me to do that; my heart grows coarser the more I hear the truth, and I grow further from you.

So how am I to know that what I hear you saying to me is really what you are saying to me and not my understanding bending the meaning of your words? If I do that when I want to kill, how can I know that I am not doing it as I argue for peace? Perhaps you want me to listen with objective ears. But there cannot be objective listening if listening means understanding and understanding involves interpretation. There is no place for me to stand outside of myself to make sure that what I hear is really what is being said. And if I am clever and talented enough, all my misinterpretations will be consistent and reinforce one another. Nor is following the consensus of your people adequate, for in this reading you tell me that they all could be wrong too.

I am left unable to trust myself and unable to trust your people, and because I can trust neither of those, I am not sure how I am supposed to trust you. Yes, you tell me the truth, but I'm not sure that's what I or your people are hearing. I feel your disappointment with me because I am treating you like some postmodern conundrum to be solved by a little more research into Derrida or Frederick Jameson. I feel you throwing up your hands: after listening to me complain for years that this or that passage was too vague for me (and no, I still don't get Revelation) and asking why you couldn't just come out and say what you meant instead of using those parables, I have found a way to doubt even what you say clearly. You have blessed me with a mind and an education that I am using against you.

I don't know where this is supposed to go next. Yes, I do understand that sometimes you have to come and fill the sanctuary with your train and the temple with smoke to scare the wits out of me so I get it right. But please, next time tone down the angels.

Bless my mind to illuminate me with your wisdom;
bless my lips to allow me to speak your word;
and bless my heart that I might live the gospel.

3

The Good Wars

Prologue

My father was proud of his service in World War II, I think. The only time he would allude to it occurred when we watched some movie or show on television that praised the Marine Corps. The Old Man always said that the Marines were overrated and benefited more from a good press office. He was in the 82nd Airborne Division, and, let me tell you, a squad of airborne was worth a battalion of . . .

But he never spoke of the war except for two times. In the winter, his hands would itch terribly, and, once, I saw him scratch them until they began to bleed. He told me they were frostbitten at the Battle of the Bulge. The only other time, I had asked him why he never drank liquor. He told me that during the war he was billeted in a house in France that had a fine wine cellar. He said he spent an evening with a bottle of brandy and got so sick that ever after he couldn't even abide the smell of alcohol. That was it. No other stories. No tales of battling Nazis or SS that I was hungry to hear some twenty years after the fact.

He died before all the shows, books, and movies about the Greatest Generation, so I am not sure what he would have made of it. I suspect not much, if he were honest. Leaving aside the part about overcoming the

Depression, which some point to as the other aspect of what made that generation great, they were praised for leaving home and work, all that was familiar and secure, in order to save the world from the ravages of Nazism and imperial Japan. They placed their lives on the line to defend our country and its values, our way of life, and they secured the freedom of oppressed peoples around the world.

I don't know how much I can generalize from the example of my father, but his story presents another side of the face of the greatest of generations. My father went into the army because he was drafted. He didn't volunteer and didn't especially want to go into the military; in fact, he told me that the only reason he ended up in the airborne was that they paid a higher monthly wage. He would laugh at the documentaries that showed the lines of young men waiting to sign up, and was as skeptical in the mid-1960s as he said he was in the '40s. Everyone he knew waited to receive his induction notice. At base he thought that Hitler was Europe's problem and no concern of ours. He never spoke of Pearl Harbor or Japan or of the America First movement, so I don't know if he was a thoroughgoing isolationist, but there were at least some other aspects of his history that I think he shared with a bit more than a small number of his fellows.

By the time I was old enough to know the difference—sometime around 1964, when I was ten years old or so—I realized that my father was a bigot, both racist and antisemitic. It was the time of the Civil Rights and Voting Rights Acts and just before the rioting that hit our cities in the late '60s. My father was heartily displeased, seeing, I suppose, African Americans' drive for equality as hurting his own prospects. "They should know their place; they are so uppity" was a sentiment I heard more than once, and in language that was much harsher. He also saw Jewish involvement in the civil rights movement as an unholy alliance. Of course, the Jews were behind it all, ruining the country; he wasn't sure that Hitler was entirely wrong. And I knew I was in deep trouble with him when he said to me, "You're like a little Jew boy . . ." I'm fairly sure it was the worst thing he could think of calling me.

Sometimes I think his bigotry was simply something abstract, if being bigoted in any way can be linked with a "simply." I remember only one of my father's friends ever coming to the house. I don't know if Karl was a Masonic Lodge brother or what else they may have had in common, but

I do know Karl was an honored guest if for no other reason than that my father kept a bottle of Clan MacGregor scotch in a sideboard to serve him. Karl was Jewish, right down to the Star of David tie tack.

And I recall many stories my father would tell me about his friend Cousin. In the '30s, before my father married, he and Cousin worked in a garage in Queen's Village, New York. It's hard for me to imagine my father having a pal, but evidently they had a great deal of fun playing pranks on coworkers and hanging out in Manhattan after work and into the small hours. After my father died, I was going through a White Owl cigar box that he always kept tucked away in his sock drawer. Aside from the normal detritus such a box holds—old car keys, broken doodads, and the like—there was a photograph of Cousin, a very large black man. I don't know what happened to Cousin or their friendship, but my father was not a sentimental man, so I figure that photo was significant.

I don't know what parts of this story of his are anomalies. It's tough to square that his only friends—or the only ones his family would ever know about—were also the objects of his race hatred. And now that I think of it, in those days he wasn't too happy about Roman Catholics either. Yet he married one and, after a time, permitted his children to be raised Catholic as well.

As we all are to a greater or lesser extent, he was a contradictory person, and perhaps his contradictions are contradictions only to his son, as mine will be to my sons. For his last fifteen years or so he found peace in an Evangelical congregation and as an old man allowed the love and gentleness that I knew so well to come much more to the surface. In those last years he was much more accepting of differences and no longer ranted about blacks, Jews, and Catholics. In fact, he bespoke a profound anguish that I was destined for hell because of my faith.

My point with this brief and painful foray into the family album is that I am not so sure the greatest generation was as great as we have made them. Apologies to Brokaw, Turkel, and Ambrose. Our parents and grandparents were as flawed as we are. They accomplished much and did much good, and they left much undone and did much evil. They defeated fascism and genocide, much as their fathers fought the war to end all wars, as their grandfathers fought to free the slaves. There is a lot of truth to those claims, and a lot of falsehood as well. Part of our responsibility as sons and daughters is trying to figure out where those strands of truth and falsity are in our own lives.

—◌◌◌—

■ I can well imagine a critic saying—especially since the critic I have in mind is charitable in interpreting my remarks—that all of the criticism of just war theory that I have gone over in the first two chapters is well and good, suitably academic and fairly well argued; there are appropriate uses of "it seems" and "appears to be the case." In fact, it even comes close to being convincing. Yet history is replete with lessons about the limitations of academic exercises, for what "appears to be the case" in the quiet and security of the ivory tower may not really be the case out there in the real world. In the real world, nations act and interact, and people of flesh and blood suffer and die in actuality rather than in abstraction. The best that can be said about a philosophical position that places the value of a critique supposedly exposing the immorality of war over and above the death of, and brutality aimed at, the uncontroversially innocent is that it is pretentious and overly idealistic. And that from a charitable critic.

The point is this: even if almost all the wars that have been fought over the millennia were wrong on both philosophical and theological grounds, there was at least one war that was not. World War II, the fight against Nazi aggression and oppression, was not only justified but was necessary. Pacifism might be what is called for in the vast majority of cases, but in this case, pacifism would be the wrong response.

It is this example that provides the genesis of the title of this book. Anyone who advocates pacifism either as a result of Christian commitment, or as a secular philosophical position, or even as a classroom exercise must provide an answer to the questions, "But what about Hitler? Isn't Hitler an example of an evil that was so great, so malignant in Germany and the conquered nations, and so menacing to the rest of the world that warfare and all it entails is the only adequate response? Doesn't the confrontation with a palpable and unquestionable evil require a different understanding of what we may and may not do?"

These are the questions Michael Walzer sets out to answer near the end of his highly praised and influential book *Just and Unjust Wars*. Through a highly rigorous and thorough examination, Walzer tries to establish the moral rules and limits that wars must follow to be considered just; essentially, he displays the contours of the just war theory I have examined, critiqued, and rejected previously. Walzer tends to be a bit more scrupulous than many other theorists in his regard for the safety and immunity of innocents. But when he considers the Hitler question, Walzer shows that he is prepared to sacrifice this principle: "Then the question is simply this: can one do *anything*, violating the rights of the innocent, in order to defeat Nazism? I am going to argue that one can indeed do what is necessary" (248–49). (John Rawls makes a similar claim and argument [see Rawls 98–015]). If the unavoidable killing of innocents is essential in war and if this provides us with very good reason to reject the claim that wars are justifiable, then Walzer's willingness to sacrifice innocents and his justification of that move in wars against extreme evil pose significant problems for peacemaking. In this chapter I will describe those certain and relevant aspects of Walzer's theory. In the next chapter I will present the reasons why I think that theory ultimately fails.

For Walzer as for many others, the Hitler regime provides the paradigmatic example of a special case that justifies using extraordinary means to defeat an enemy, what he calls "the supreme emergency." Even though I reject his version of just war theory as merely another variant of a morally untenable position, his discussion of supreme emergencies cuts right to the point of this book, since it offers the clearest account of the exception to the rules, both secular and Christian. If Walzer is correct, then even if pacifism is normally mandated, there come times when it must be abandoned.

Walzer is surely correct when he states that the notion of a supreme emergency is used too often by political leaders in order to justify conflicts that are not emergencies, let alone supreme ones. Too frequently it is a rhetorical device used to motivate the citizenry or military to even greater efforts and sacrifice. But there is a valid sense in which "supreme emergency" is used to justify whatever means necessary to defeat an enemy:

> [The meaning of "supreme emergency"] is defined by two criteria, which correspond to the two levels on which the concept of necessity works: the first has to do with the imminence of the danger and the second with its nature.... Then we are offered what might best be called the back-to-the-wall argument: that when conventional means of resistance are hopeless or worn out, anything goes (anything that is "necessary" to win). (252)

Walzer is very careful to focus on the *supreme* importance of victory. Many interactions that nations engage in may involve some amount of danger, and the prospect of defeat by an enemy may also be imminent. But what a state risks by defeat must be subjected to a comprehensive analysis:

What is it that defeat entails? Is it some minor territorial adjustment, a loss of face (for the leaders), the payment of heavy indemnities, political reconstruction of this or that sort, the surrender of national independence, the exile or murder of millions of people? In such cases, one's back is always to the wall, but the dangers one confronts take very different forms, and the different forms make a difference. (252–53)

It is obvious that the difference among these different forms of danger to a state involve various levels of seriousness. A minor territorial adjustment may well be more appropriately dealt with through negotiation, and a loss of face by a diminution of pride rather than by even limited wars. But as the list goes on, the fear, anxiety, and desperation of the target state rise concomitantly. Not all dangers are equal, and the greater the danger, the more extreme should be the response to it. Walzer elaborates this point and begins his discussion of Hitler and Nazism:

We need to make a map of human crises and to mark off the regions of desperation and disaster. These and only these constitute the realm of necessity, truly understood. . . . Nazism lies at the outer limits of exigency, at a point where we are likely to find ourselves united in fear and abhorrence.

That is what I am going to assume, at any rate, on behalf of all those people who believed at the time and still believe a third of a century later that Nazism was an ultimate threat to everything decent in our lives, an ideology and a practice of domination so murderous, so degrading even to those who might survive, that the consequences of its final victory were literally beyond calculation, immeasurably awful. We see it—and I don't use the phrase lightly—as evil objectified in the world, and in a form so potent and apparent that there could never have been anything to do but to fight against it. . . . Here was a threat to human values so radical that its imminence would surely constitute a supreme emergency. (253)

This description certainly seems correct, and I cannot fault Walzer's characterization of the Nazi regime as possessing an ideology and practice of horror and degradation. But if Nazism is to serve as the paradigm for that section of the map that is the extremity—that area where warfare may be unleashed with few if any constraints against an implacable enemy who embodies evil—then we need to be more specific. What is it precisely about the spread of Nazism that constitutes a supreme emergency? If this is to be a useful benchmark to decide when killing is unquestionably justified, then it must be framed in terms that can be applied to other situations at other times and in a manner that severely limits controversy. What Walzer

68

is advocating is the major challenge to pacifists in general and to Christians in particular: that in times of supreme emergency the rules of peace must be broken, and the rights of neutrals, innocents, and noncombatants can, under the right circumstances, be overridden, *"and when we override them we make no claim that they have been diminished, weakened or lost."* (247, emphasis added)

Let me be very clear: even if just war theory is fatally flawed, Walzer is putting forth a case that purports to take precedence over our moral and religious prohibitions against killing, and he goes further, to assert that even the lives of the innocent may be sacrificed, with justification, in the case of supreme emergencies. This is of crucial importance, because even just war theorists deny that it is ever justifiable to kill the innocent directly and intentionally. In fact, the direct and intentional violation of the rights of innocents is taken as a primary reason that some wars are unjust and should never be waged under those circumstances.

Now, it is very difficult to understand his statement that the rights of innocents and others may be overridden with no assertion that those rights have been lost or diminished. So difficult is it to understand that I am prone to argue that his claim makes no sense at all. The notion of rights, if it has any meaning at all, demarcates those areas that should *not* be overridden. I think it is obvious that Walzer does not admit the existence of absolute rights—that is, rights that should not be overridden under any circumstances—because it is hard to imagine what those rights might be in the flow and structure of his discussion. If all rights are, therefore, contextualized such that any of them may be overridden given the correct circumstances, then, just as clearly, those rights do not exist under those circumstances.

To put it another way, let us assume, as Walzer and most of us do, that an innocent person has a right to life. If Walzer is correct, then there are circumstances that legitimate the taking of the life of that innocent person. If taking the life of the innocent person is legitimate, then that person does not have a right to life in those circumstances. If, on the other hand, Walzer means that the taking of the innocent's life is legitimate *and* the innocent retains her right to life in an undiminished way, then I have absolutely no idea what Walzer could be saying. It is incoherent to assert that it is both right and wrong to kill the innocent.

But, in fact, Walzer does assert something of this sort. He maintains that in a supreme emergency one must wager the "determinate crime (the killing of innocent people) against that immeasurable evil (a Nazi triumph)" (259). He goes on to say that the action stands as a crime even though necessary to victory; it is necessary to maintain the inviolability of rights because it holds the key to our common future. But I dare to say that our history will be nullified and our future condemned unless I accept the burdens of criminality here and now. (260)

I just do not know what to make of this kind of reasoning—that it may be necessary to violate rights in order to preserve their inviolability, and that it is a crime to do so even though the alternative is so much worse that it is mandatory to commit the crime. This leaves us with no understanding of what we should do or how we should evaluate the actions of others. I think it is much more honest to assert what seems to be obvious: that if an innocent is killed and that killing is justified by recourse to supreme emergency, her right to life has been lost or forfeited.

I am not trying to score debating points against Walzer or those who share his view. I am trying to take them seriously, and the stakes involved are enormous. This doctrine of supreme emergency is the key for distinguishing a class of wars that, proponents argue, must be fought out of necessity. We need to be very clear about what such a doctrine entails and not try to soften its implications with nonsensical platitudes.

Nor do I wish to imply that Walzer regards the rights of innocents in a cavalier manner. For Walzer, rights are not petty inconveniences that may be ignored with impunity. Indeed, I think it is precisely because Walzer respects rights so much that he creates the bizarre formulation of overriding them while at the same time preserving them. So, even though Walzer is willing to sanction performing whatever action is necessary to defeat a threat that is a supreme emergency, the "overriding of rights" may occur only as a last resort, not for convenience or simple utility. It stands as a justified act of criminality.

The utility he espouses is not simple, but it is there nonetheless. Since the notion of supreme emergency is so important to the issues we are examining, we need to clarify its outlines as much as possible. Walzer puts forward the following questions and answers:

> Can a supreme emergency be constituted by a particular threat—by a threat of enslavement or extermination directed against a single nation? Can soldiers and statesmen override the rights of innocent people for the sake of their own political community? I am inclined to answer this question affirmatively, though not without hesitation and worry. What choice do they have? They might sacrifice themselves in order to uphold the moral law, but they cannot sacrifice their countrymen. Faced with some absolute horror, their options exhausted, they will do what they must to save their own people. (254)

This notion of saving one's own people is crucial, and Walzer's meaning is clear, at least with the example of extermination. If one's fellow citizens are liable to be massacred by the threat, then whatever means necessary to prevent that would be mandated. The "threat of enslavement" and "acting for the sake of [one's] political community" are considerably more obscure.

Ancient history is replete with examples of empires extending their realms and carrying off whole populations of conquered peoples to serve as slaves for the wealthy and powerful. It is not so clear what the contemporary equivalent of enslavement of a nation means. While the Germans did round up Jews and other targeted groups in conquered nations and use them as slave laborers in the work camps and factories of Germany, they did not do that to the dominant populations of conquered countries. The Nazis did subordinate those countries' political institutions to their own governance and did appropriate some measure of the nations' goods, valuables (such as artworks), and labor for their own purposes.

Clearly, German rule was oppressive, and many innocents died, but it seems that the relevant aspect of a criterion for supreme emergency that Walzer is underscoring lies less with the appropriation of some measure of a nation's goods and services and much more with the elimination or subordination of political institutions. At least, I think that is the aspect of enslavement that Walzer wants to stress. Britain, Walzer's prime example of a state confronting a supreme emergency, did not face the prospect of the wholesale slaughter of its entire civilian population—no state conquered by the Germans suffered that fate. Nor did the British face enslavement in the classical, ancient sense. Many nations have been forced to pay large indemnities after losing a war—Germany in 1918 and France in 1871 are two examples. So the appropriation of money or labor does not seem to be sufficient for enslavement in Walzer's sense. What we are left with, then, is the very real prospect that the German victory over Britain would result in the destruction of the British political community.

Walzer addresses the centrality of the issue of the survival of the community when he states:

> For the survival and freedom of political communities—whose members share a way of life, developed by their ancestors, to be passed on to their children—are the highest values of international society. Nazism challenged these values on a grand scale, but challenges more narrowly conceived, *if they are of the same kind,* have similar moral consequences. They bring us under the rule of necessity (and necessity knows no rules). (254)

Since Walzer's notion of enslavement refers to this kind of phenomenon, we can restate the conditions for a supreme emergency that would justify not only conventional warfare but also total war: the existence of an imminent threat of the extinction of an entire people (genocide) or of the annihilation of the right of self-determination for a political community.

It is important to note at this juncture that this formulation of the conditions for a supreme emergency applies not only to threats directed against one's own state but also to third-party states, nations, and ethnic or religious groups. The idea of a supreme emergency could be used to justify a bystander state's intervention in the internal affairs of another state if the latter is engaged in a genocidal policy, such as Rwanda; or an intervention in a cross-border conflict where genocide is occurring or threatened, such as Serbian involvement in Bosnia. Thus, the war against Hitler and Nazism was a supreme emergency on both grounds: the Nazi policy of exterminating Jews and other groups within their territory satisfies the criteria, and German expansionism, which eliminated the right of self-determination for the independent political communities they invaded, also justifies it.

It is very difficult to determine with any precision when a supreme emergency begins or when it ends, even retrospectively. Walzer makes it very clear in his exposition that, from the standpoint of Britain alone, a condition of supreme emergency probably existed only from 1940 until 1942, when German military prowess was at its highest and appeared unstoppable, and the threat to Britain was imminent. Thus, while any action necessary to defeat Germany was sanctioned during that time, events such as the firebombing of Dresden in the spring of 1945—resulting in the deaths of over 100,000 persons—were not justified.

It is even harder to determine the beginning and the end of the supreme emergency posed by the Holocaust. While the passage of the Nuremberg Laws in 1936 seems too early for the supreme emergency entailed by the genocide that was to follow later, those laws did annihilate the political right of self-determination for a well-defined group of people, so it would seem that a sufficient condition for a supreme emergency would arise soon thereafter. It does seem clearer that the genocide condition would be satisfied at the latest with the Wannsee Conference of January 1942, when the plans for the implementation of the Final Solution for Europe were finalized. We must remember that actual killing need not have occurred; the existence of an imminent threat of extermination is what is required. And the genocide condition would seem to have persisted as long as the death camps were in operation carrying out the policy of the government: for while Germany ceased to be an imminent threat to the political communities of Europe by 1943, it retained its threatening status vis-à-vis the Jews of occupied Europe right up to the end of the war and the liberation of the camps. Thus, if one could make a credible case that the firebombing of Dresden was necessary, not as a means of halting Nazi threats to the safety of Europe, but rather as a means to halt the murder of Jews and other non-Aryans, the destruction of Dresden—as well as the other civilian targets in the Allied campaign of terror bombing—would be justified.

It must also be said that events and situations tend not to be as clear in real time as they are in retrospect. It is difficult, even after the fact sometimes, to determine what constitutes a supreme threat and when disaster is imminent. Even though some aspects may be murky, we have achieved some measure of clarity now, just over sixty years after the end of the Second World War, and there is great value in examining that war as a guide to future actions. Nonetheless, judgments are always difficult, and our weighing of relevant factors is always prone to error. We must grant decision makers a certain amount of leeway for mistakes in their analyses and policy decisions: precision is not always attainable, even in retrospect.

It is because historians and theorists have gained some measure of clarity on the circumstances and conditions that make World War II the paradigm of the Good War that it occupies such a central place in our reasoning about and evaluation of warfare. It provides theorists and policy makers with relevant tools of analysis and historical precedent, for if World War II was not only justifiable but mandatory and the prime example of the Good War that must be fought, then any international circumstance that is relevantly similar to World War II demands relevantly similar actions as a response.

This yields what I will call the Hitler Test, or the Hitlerization of politics. When policy makers of various governments try to determine whether and how to intervene in international occurrences, they either explicitly or implicitly apply the conditions pertinent to the situation of Germany under the Nazis. For all the ambiguities that might exist regarding the Third Reich, the evil that the German nation perpetrated on subject peoples is clear enough to provide an indispensable standard for military intervention. Therefore, we can easily justify Viet Nam's invasion of Cambodia to stop the slaughter of the killing fields; and advisers made the argument to President Clinton that Slobodan Milošević was a Serbian Hitler pursuing a genocidal policy against Muslims and Albanians, an argument that led to the NATO bombing of Serbia. And the second Bush administration had dubbed Saddam Hussein as a Hitler, and his regime Nazi-like, not only for the threat they posed to all nations of the world but also for oppressive and genocidal policies they pursued internally.

Some applications of the Hitler Test and the Hitlerization of enemies seem appropriate, while others appear more questionable. Idi Amin, Mu'ammar Gadhafi, "Papa Doc" Duvalier, Kim Il Sung, and his son Kim Jung Il as well as many others have been labeled as Hitlers, and while all of those so labeled are or have been tyrants and nasty people, it is simply not clear that each and every one of them personify evil in the way that Hitler does. We have a similar problem with the application of the term *genocide*. It is often said that the state of Israel is pursuing a genocidal policy against the Palestinians. Such a claim appears on its face to be hyperbolic. Even if one were to judge Israeli policies to be oppressive of Palestinians and violative of their fundamental right of self-determination, it is simply a gross exaggeration to label those policies genocidal. Even in domestic, criminal judgments we tend to Hitlerize a certain class of malefactors, implicitly by using the same terms we use to characterize Hitler. Thus, John Wayne Gacy, Jeffrey Dahmer, and Timothy McVeigh, to name just three, have all been called personifications of evil.

There seem to be two sides to this proliferation of Hitlerization. On the one hand, it seems that we are becoming more sensitive to or appreciative of the extremity involved in warfare or the application of the death penalty. As we recognize the severity of those actions, we are less inclined to use them precipitously. We congratulate ourselves that we appear to have reached the point where we are more inclined to use them in limited circumstances—only for those imminent threats to all those things we most value.

On the other hand, it also seems that Hitlerization serves the opposite effect, that is, expanding the number of violent responses we make to international and domestic disturbances. The more we call leaders of other nations "Hitler" or speak of policies as "genocidal" or characterize criminals as "the personification of evil," the more our legitimate response to those people and events are constrained. We must respond to them with extreme measures, or else we are not performing our moral duty to defend ourselves, our political community, or other innocents who are threatened victims. Hitlerization and the supreme emergencies that arise from it have no alternatives. The problem is that it is very difficult to discern which applications of Hitlerization are accurate and which are not, when nations are facing supreme emergencies and when they are not.

It seems that today the people of the United States have reached some sort of consensus that America is facing a Hitler in Osama bin Laden and a supreme emergency with the rise of Al Qaeda and Islamicist* terrorism. International terrorism of the kind Al Qaeda engages in poses particular problems for framing a justified response.

Islamicist terrorism is a very different form of terrorism than we have seen since the Second World War. The standard models of terrorist organizations do not seem to fit an organization like Al Qaeda. The Irish Republican Army in Britain, the FLN of Algeria, the Stern Gang of British Palestine, Shining Path of Peru, Hamas in Lebanon and the West Bank, and on and on—each of these groups used terrorist tactics for nationalistic purposes against what they claimed were oppressive governments or colonial rulers. As such, the governments they attacked through their terror campaigns could characterize them and treat them as domestic threats to peace, security, and legitimate sovereignty. In short, they could be regarded as criminals and pursued under the aegis of the police function states possess. As we have seen, states have a wide latitude in the way they choose to respond to internal violations of law and, essentially, answer to no one but the citizenry in the pursuit of their domestic policies.

The problem of Islamicist terrorists in general and Al Qaeda in particular is precisely their international character. When they destroyed the World Trade Center on September 11, 2001, and killed 3,000 people, it wasn't very clear what kind of response was justified. In other words, before we could figure out what steps we could take in response to that action, we needed to figure out what the action was. Timothy McVeigh's terror bombing of the Federal Building in Oklahoma City, for example, posed no such problem. We understood, as soon as the investigation was completed, that we were dealing with a criminal act of domestic terrorism, and our law enforcement mechanisms and structures provided the appropriate means of response.

While the destruction of the World Trade Center was a domestic occurrence, the perpetrators of the act were all foreign nationals and part of a supranational entity; thus, it had some features of a domestic criminal act and some features of an act of war. Yet, because the members of Al Qaeda were not representatives or agents of other sovereign nations, the act does not quite seem to fit the model of what a war is either. To contrast it with another case, the attack on Pearl Harbor was similarly surprising and destructive, but we could identify it as an act of war by another sovereign state. The United States, therefore, did not consider that act as one of domestic criminality but rather as an occasion to resort to international warfare.

* *Islamicist* is a term used to distinguish radical Muslim fundamentalists from other Muslim groups pressing political agendas.

The problem is a significant one. If the World Trade Center bombing was an act of criminality, the legal jurisdiction of the United States ends at its borders. While the United States government could do whatever it determined was legal within its borders, it would have to necessarily rely on the willing cooperation of other sovereign states to pursue and prosecute the other criminals involved. If the World Trade Center bombing was an act of war, on the other hand, the United States would be justified in prosecuting its war response across borders and treat the perpetrators not as criminals, whose civil rights are intact prior to conviction, but as enemy combatants who are subject to the rules of war. Even though I believe that the justification of a state's police power is ultimately derived from just war theory and therefore contains serious difficulties for Christian pacifists, I also think that this change in the way we regard terrorism might alter the way we think to respond to it, one that might be more peaceful. For example, most industrialized nations, as well at the Catholic Church, hold that the execution of criminals is morally unjustifiable, whereas neither of those groups holds the same opinion about international warfare.

This problem forces us to consider what international terrorism is. More specifically, we need to examine the claim made by the United States administration—a claim that many Americans seem to agree with—not only that the United States is engaged in a war with international terrorism but also that the threat posed by Al Qaeda and its allies is a threat to our survival. In short, that September 11 has initiated a condition of supreme emergency.

Fourth Meditation

1 Corinthians 5:9–13

In my letter, I wrote to you that you should have nothing to do with people living immoral lives. I was not including everybody in this present world who is sexually immoral, or everybody who is greedy, or dishonest or worships false gods—that would mean you would have to cut yourselves off completely from the world. In fact what I meant was that you were not to have anything to do with anyone going by the name of brother who is sexually immoral, or is greedy, or worships false gods, or is a slanderer or a drunkard or dishonest; never even have a meal with anybody of that kind. It is no concern of mine to judge outsiders. It is for you to judge those who are inside, is it not? But outsiders are for God to judge.

You must banish this evil-doer from among you.

■ Lord, help me to remember I am always in your presence.

Right off the bat, Lord, I have to ask you how this fits with the consolation passages. I am thinking of "Judge not lest you be judged" and "Let him among you who is without sin cast the first stone." I call them consolation passages because they seem to take me off the hook both ways: they give a ready response to those who are judging me, and they relieve me of the unpleasant job of calling others to task. Yes, it does make for a nice conspiracy of silence, but I'd rather not think about the downsides right now. Instead, let's look at the pluses. I understood you to be cautioning me about self-righteousness and arrogance, considering myself so much better than others that I could actually fit in your position as judge. That, frankly, has always frightened me more than being called to account.

But in this passage you are telling me to shun the sinner. No, Paul did not say "sinner," but that's how I took it. He is, after all, talking about people living immoral lives. So perhaps the person he's talking about isn't just a sinner like we all are, but one who persists in the sin and cannot even see that it is a sinful life he or she is leading. I wonder if that is a legitimate distinction, that is, between one who sins and one who leads an immoral life. I guess I blend the two, thinking that my sinning is the leading of an immoral life, if for no other reason than the quantity of sin in my life. It's a bit off topic, Lord, but I'm looking this over and am surprised how easily I admit being a sinner, surprised because if anyone actually did call me to account because of my sins, I know I would emphatically deny them. As a matter of fact, whenever I consider my sins I'm not sure I'm actually considering them sinful, if you know what I mean. So much seems formulaic and not reality; it's as though I couldn't face the reality very often.

But back to the passage, most of the descriptions Paul uses refer to what the immoral person is and not really to what he or she does. He points to one who *is* sexually immoral or *is* greedy. The only action Paul specifies is "worships false gods." I worry now that I am philosophizing instead of praying, parsing and chopping the language, looking so closely at the details that I am missing the message you want me to get.

I think you are dragging me toward the verse that tells me I should not cut myself off from the world that does not follow the Way, the folks who are outside the church. This is an odd message to me and vaguely discomfiting: we should have nothing to do with Christians leading immoral lives, but we should be engaged with non-Christians leading immoral lives. I am not sure what the difference is supposed to mean, because it seems to me that we should bring your Word to those who do not believe, yes, but also to those who only say they believe. It's the lost sheep thing, Lord, you know, another consolation passage, remember? More rejoicing in heaven over the return of one who has strayed than the ninety-nine who have stayed? So I thought we were to try to bring them back. Or is this some kind of disciplinary thing, that no one should have even the outward sign of fellowship in the church unless she is trying to reform her life? But it still seems too harsh to have *nothing* to do with her.

Perhaps what's at the root of this is that hypocrisy is contagious. Maybe to be a successful hypocrite one has to be adept at rationalizing, making some kind of acceptable justification for the falsehood he wants so badly to believe. We can weave these wonderful psychological or theological arguments to support immorality because to face the truth would make it impossible for us to look ourselves in the eye and impossible for us to persist in what we want to do against your word.

So then the problem lies in making those arguments plausible. As the hypocrite convinces herself so can she convince others, and she has to convince others to protect herself in her fictions. And maybe that's what's happening to me as I sit down to write about terrorism. It seems funny to say it like this, but terror scares me. My insignificance has protected me from all sorts of attack, and it is that insignificance that invites the terrorist. In order to protect myself I create the hypocritical fictions of philosophy and theology, and weave these wonderful fabrics of justification; and I seek out others who argue and weave better than I do so I can get some cover, so to speak.

So is it a way of preserving the church that we should shun the immoral believer, giving us some insulation from a twisted and twisting logic? Then that also means that those living immoral lives outside the church are safer to be around, because at least they are not hypocrites. Those immoralists are living honest lives of dishonesty. Those folk we should not judge, but our brothers and sisters we should, and ourselves as well.

I can't pretend that I am getting this entirely. I understand calling one another to account and telling one another, in a very specific and uncomfortable way, that we can live better than we are. I think I understand the power of speaking truth, even though I find it hard to do so, because to speak the truth is to speak you. So what I do not understand is how the banishment of the evildoer from among us fits with any of this. Are we really that safe from the arguments of the pagans that the power of speaking truth and calling one another to account is enough? But then why would neither be efficacious with the evildoer in our midst?

I am having trouble accepting this; it doesn't seem to make much sense. Let me try to take it more inward and to heart, make it less an abstract and remote theological problem.

Is it in some sense better when I sin knowing that I am sinning, saying to myself, "I know this is wrong, but I am going to do it anyway" than when I rationalize the sin? It looks like rationalizing the sin is sinning twice—the sin itself is evil, and selling myself a story that tries to make it acceptable to me is a sin as well. But that seems never to work. I don't believe my rationalizations. I know I am lying to myself and, therefore, am never successful in believing the lie because I do know that it is false. So I guess the real question is whether there are any times that I manage to believe the lie I tell myself—and that's a question I just cannot answer. If I believe the lie, then I have managed to transform it into what I think is true; so its falseness becomes inaccessible just as soon as I believe it. And in addition to this, in order for it to be a successful false belief, everything else that I believe to be true must be shaved and fitted to conform to the falsehood. Then it's likely that many of my beliefs, if not all of them, become tainted in order to accommodate the falsehood I have sold myself. I can't get out of this hole.

So, is that why you say the church must judge? The only way for me to uncover the falsehoods that make the life I live immoral is for others to uncover it, because I am stuck in the hole. Others must uncover it, judge it, and banish me if I will not see the truth. It isn't the arcane philosophical principle or the abstract theological insight that are the things I should fear in my prayer, or fear will infect the church. The focus we should have is on the life a believer lives. Denying the truth by living a life of falsehood is a life of denying you, and those who deny you are outside the church. Banishment, then, is merely the living of the truth.

Merely. Doesn't seem to be anything "merely" about this.

Bless my mind to illuminate me with your wisdom;
bless my lips to allow me to speak your word;
and bless my heart that I might live the gospel.

4

Terror

Prologue

I loved the time I spent working in soup kitchens, especially when I was in my early twenties. There was a reality there that I have found nowhere else, a community that is hard to describe. It is also hard for me to recall a time when I was more embarrassed and humbled than after my first week in my first soup kitchen. I was mopping up vomit from the floor of the dining area when the supervisor of the place called me aside and told me they didn't need me any more. I was surprised and pointed out that the place was terribly understaffed and was constantly looking for help, so I didn't understand why I wasn't needed. She looked me in the eye and told me that what they needed were workers who would look upon the homeless, the addicted, and the drunk as human beings, that they needed workers who realized that the ones being helped were the workers themselves.

I began to get it then, a beginning I repeated often. It was a forgiving place.

One night a few years later I was working the night shift in another soup kitchen in New England, getting the beds ready in the dormitory. Two men entered the dorm from the hallway, arguing. One of them was O'Grady, whom everyone called Rosie. No surprise that there was an argument. Rosie was a bitter and unpleasant man when sober and unspeakably nasty when drunk; he held the Kitchen record for getting tossed out. This night he had a full bag on and was abusing one of the nicest, gentlest guys who came by. Rabbit was of the Abenaki tribe and always had a smile, was always pleasant even when he was getting scrubbed with Rid-X to get clean of lice. But on that night Rabbit wasn't smiling.

I tried to distract them, to defuse things as they walked around checking the beds out, but Rosie would have none of it. As Rosie was turning his venom on me, out of the corner of my eye I saw that Rabbit had pulled a butcher knife from his coat. More men were beginning to come in, and I heard someone say, "Uh oh." Under my breath I swore at the idiot worker on the door who was supposed to be checking for bottles and weapons before he let the men into the Kitchen for the night. And then I did something very stupid. I decided to take Rabbit down.

This was stupid for many reasons. There were occasional fights in the dorm, but there were always two of us workers there to break it up, and the idiot on the door hadn't come up into the dorm yet. Second, I was a real skinny guy who had never played football, and an academic at heart even then. So while I had mastered the theory of the chop block at the knees, I had no practical idea how to take out a guy twice my size. The third reason this was stupid was that, when sober, Rabbit worked high iron; he was a construction worker in Boston who routinely walked steel girders many stories high on work sites. There was no way he was going to fall down even if I knew how to do it.

But all of this is on reflection. I threw myself at Rabbit's knees and accomplished nothing but making him angrier. He pulled me up by the neck, held me against the wall, and put the point of the butcher knife against my ribs. He announced, "We're having ground beef for supper tomorrow."

At that point I figured it was over. No one was going to intervene— they all had too much sense—and my hunch was that Rosie was coveting my shoes. Resistance was out of the question. I was pinned with my feet off the floor like some pale, bearded butterfly. So I did the only thing I could think of: I gave Rabbit permission. "You can kill me, Rabbit."

"Why did you attack me, Brimlow? Rosie your friend?"

"No, Rabbit. I don't like him either."

"I just wanted to scare him. Shut him up."

"Well, Rabbit, works for me."

The smile came back. He put me down and told me I was a good boy. Rabbit left and I never saw him again. Rosie was quiet the rest of the night, and I retched.

———※———

■ It cannot be disputed that the events of September 11 as well as the acts of terror directed against American embassies prior to that date exhibit the fact that the United States is being threatened by forces that lie outside of American territorial control. The key questions we need to examine are:

- Why are we being attacked?
- What is being threatened?
- How should we respond to it?

In her fascinating book *Just War against Terror*, Jean Bethke Elshtain offers one of the first of what I assume will be many analyses of the phenomenon facing the United States, and I will take her discussion of these issues as emblematic of the primary trends of reflection in the country.

In the introduction of her book, Elshtain lays out in rough outline what she takes the issues to be. Within the first two pages, Elshtain discusses the difficulty some persons in contemporary society have in recognizing and dealing with evil:

> In modernity, it simply must be the case that all human purposes and the means deployed to achieve them are open to adjudication and argument. Just get the aggrieved parties to really talk to one another, because that is the way reasonable people do things. (1)

Elshtain goes on to argue that, while this outlook that reasonable people can and will negotiate to solve their grievances and complaints may work in many spheres, it is alien, futile, and ultimately dangerous when a society is confronted by objectified evil.

Like Walzer, Elshtain's primary example of this is Nazism. No amount of negotiation, concession, or appeasement was or could have been useful in bringing to an end the evil of Germany in the 1930s and 1940s. As she puts it, while we need to be cognizant of the social and political conditions from which Nazism arose, and need to take account of the way the Allied powers of the First World War exacerbated those conditions, none of it serves to explain, much less excuse, the evil of Nazism.

> The overriding truth and most salient fact of National Socialism is simply stated: A group of people took over state power, aimed to expand the Aryan Empire through ruthless force, and, as dictated by their ideology of biological racism, murdered whole categories of people not because of anything they had done but because of who they were. (2)

With this passage, Elshtain establishes the central theses necessary for her to offer a justification for a war against terrorism. By establishing that Osama bin Laden, Al Qaeda, and other Islamicist terrorists are embodiments of evil similar to the Nazis, Elshtain can proceed to argue that no amount of negotiation or accommodation of their views will serve to end the violence they bring to the United States and other Western democracies. To take one example, bin Laden as well as 120 Saudi intellectuals claim that there is a causal relationship between American foreign policy—including having troops in Saudi Arabia—and the September 11 attack. Elshtain interprets their comments to mean that if the United States "sought to withdraw from the world outside its borders and removed its hand from inflammatory issues," the Islamicist terrorists as well as the Muslim world would leave us in peace. (6)

In response, Elshtain argues that it is impossible for the United States to withdraw and establish a policy of isolationism. Even if we could alter our foreign policy to a status it came close to having in the nineteenth century and the years between the world wars—an isolationism that somehow included Latin America and the Philippines—it is not so clear that the United States has the ability to halt the spread of its cultural values, both good and bad, from the world. In addition, America is unable to make its financial transactions and economic structures pertain only to domestic affairs. The world has grown too interdependent, especially with globalization, and it is too easy to transmit movies, music, and television with even the current status of telecommunications. Elshtain's focus, however, is not centered so much on the practical difficulties involved in this kind of withdrawal from world affairs. Her argument rests upon the moral obligation the United States has to combat evil wherever it exists.

She argues first that American isolationism rightly ended with the war against the Nazis and Japanese imperialism. She maintains that the great military and economic power that the United States possesses entails that this nation has a concomitant responsibility to maintain a right order in the world. As she says, "Victims of genocide, for example, have a reasonable expectation that powerful nations devoted to human rights will attempt to stay the hands of their murderers" (6). She caps this argument with the assertion that international civic peace requires that the United States maintain its values; without the exercise of American power, the spread of terrorism, the death of innocents, and the threat to basic human rights will continue unabated.

But Elshtain's other argument is even more compelling and provides the foundation for the argument I've cited above. Elshtain argues that even if it were possible for the United States to withdraw from international affairs in the way that she says the Islamicist terrorists want, it would make no difference. "When I claim that changes in our policies would not satisfy Islamicists, the reason is quite basic: they loathe us because of who we are and what our society represents" (3). More substantively, she claims that bin Laden and all those who share his views are intent on the complete destruction of Americans and all the social values we prize in ourselves and are committed to foster for all people. Essentially we value the principle of freedom—that all people everywhere may be free to determine for themselves their present as well as their future, and do so in an atmosphere and polity of peace and security. Injustice is whatever violates this basic freedom all people possess.

In this brief outline contained in the introduction—an outline that is further elaborated and supported in the body of the text—Elshtain provides an answer to the three questions I posed at the beginning of this chapter. The United States and all Western democracies are being attacked by Islamicist terrorists because they hate us. This hatred arises from their degenerate understanding of the dictates of Islam, which they believe condemns infidels. Second, they are threatening our lives with murder and our way of life and most precious beliefs and values with extinction. Third, the way we should respond is by waging war, to protect ourselves and our American polity, but also to preserve the peace and security of the world and assure the right to self-determination for all peoples.

In light of the discussion at the end of the previous chapter, Elshtain's response is very interesting. At the end of the previous chapter I posed a problem for our current war on terrorism: since the war model seems to assume the existence of antagonistic states, isn't it more appropriate to consider the actions of Al Qaeda and other terrorists to be criminal rather than aggressive in the traditional sense? While she doesn't quite address this issue directly, Elshtain does seem to answer the question in two ways. In one section of her argument she is focusing on that part of just war theory that sanctions a state's intervention in the affairs of another state in order to preserve civic order (see, for example, 166–67). In another section of her argument (e.g., 162–64), Elshtain criticizes the view that the September 11 attacks be treated as criminal cases by international juridical bodies, precisely because those courts and tribunals, such as the International Criminal Court, lack a structural accountability, do not have a body of precedents to guide their decisions, and are not rooted in general legitimacy and consent. The concerns regarding justice that these courts are supposed to address are best left to independent national states. With this strand of her argument, Elshtain seems in many ways to return to a more Augustinian notion of just war theory where there is no bright-line division between a state's right to wage a just war and a state's right to exercise police powers. Let us recall that at the time Augustine wrote, the Roman Empire's military served both the contemporary function of an army as well as that of a police force. By eliminating the distinction—or at least by making the distinction a blurry one—Elshtain manages to outline a pathway to solve the problem of the last chapter.

It should be clear by this point that I think Elshtain has assembled significant reasons to justify waging war against Islamicist terrorism. She makes a case that the United States has just cause to fight the war based upon both self-defense grounds and the threat to the basic human dignity of citizens of other countries. The intention of the United States in these circumstances is to establish peace and security in the international sphere and to maintain justice. Finally, regarding the last condition I will consider, this war is taking place as a last resort: there are no other possible options open to the United States in order to resolve these issues given the single-minded and pathological hatred the terrorists have for non-Muslims.

More than simply showing that the war against terrorism is a just war, I believe Elshtain has also provided the foundation for considering this a case of supreme emergency as Walzer defines it. Bin Laden passes the Hitler test. Hitler killed the Jews not for what they had done but because of who they were; Al Qaeda wants to kill us not for what we have done but for who we are. The Islamicist terrorists are not only engaging in a genocidal activity but also posing an imminent threat to the survival of our political community, domestically as well as globally.

The World Trade Center attacks and the threat of further attacks place the values by which we define ourselves at risk. There is not only the material threat that governmental officials will be assassinated and political structures endangered, but there is the further threat that, in an attempt to defeat the terrorists, more and more of the freedoms Americans enjoy will be constrained or, ultimately, eliminated. Terrorism, by its nature, endangers in many ways the values that mark our political community as distinctive.

Regarding globalism, the story is a bit more complicated. As Elshtain expresses it,

> The internal infrastructures of particular civil societies are connected to their counterparts in other societies in many ways. Civil society of this international sort is not possible without the domestic peace provided by states. If states do not afford ordinary civic peace, there is no civil society, hence nothing to connect to externally. (161)

In other words, insofar as we have and are continuing to build toward a more comprehensive and inclusive international society, those who have the military power and political will must eliminate threats to the civic order. In this passage Elshtain eliminates the distinction between police powers and just war, in favor of just war. The situation she describes is analogous to the maintenance of civic order in all the neighborhoods of a city. It is impossible to contain either the material destruction or moral harms when one neighborhood's peace and security degrade into lawlessness and violence. Since we should desire to maintain peace and stability so that the entire community shall flourish, we must engage any and all threats; to do otherwise constitutes a threat to the viability of the whole.

I think that the perception that the world, not just the West, is facing a supreme emergency is also borne out by the rhetoric of American political leaders as well as the governments of other nations. That judgment is further confirmed by the actions these states are taking. There are numerous instances of the deprivation of the rights of innocents, such as the imprisonment of Afghans, Iraqis, Americans, and others for years before they were released because the evidence of their "enemy combatant" status proved wanting. There are frequent allegations of the sanctioned torture of suspected terrorists, and discussions in the United States Supreme Court about "ticking bomb" scenarios indicate that we are considering torture as a viable means of interrogation. There are precedents for such curtailment of rights, even in domestic American history: Lincoln, for example, suspended *habeas corpus*—which some would argue is the most basic right Americans possess—during the Civil War and placed the Supreme Court under virtual house arrest. As we have seen with Michael Walzer's reasoning regarding supreme emergencies, even more serious violations of basic rights would be permitted if rational analysis of the circumstances dictated that they were necessary measures to eliminate the imminent threats to the political community.

Thus far I have examined Elshtain's analysis of the reasons why bin Laden and the Islamicist terrorists are at war with us and her claims for the justice of our military response to the threat they pose to the polity of the United States and the international world order. There is another part to the general argument against all terrorist organizations, however, which maintains that the methodology they employ in prosecuting war is as unjust as their causes tend to be. What is it about terrorist actions in themselves in this contemporary era that makes them wrong, for even to call an act "terrorist" is to indicate that we consider it to be immoral? In order to begin this examination, though, we have to reach some kind of understanding about what terrorist acts are in order to figure out what aspect of them makes them wrong.

Our first stopping place is ordinary usage; the class of actions that ordinary people label as terrorism is as likely a candidate as any other to aid our understanding. This turns out not to be much help, because it appears that we often use the term to indicate instances of mass murder. This is not quite right, because whatever we may think of Sammy "the Bull" Gravano and David Berkowitz—the first, a mob hit man with nineteen admitted murders; the other, a serial killer—neither should be thought of as terrorists. Nor does terrorism necessarily involve killing. Hijacking airplanes or ocean liners is often called terrorist, even if no one dies in the process.

The missing element that those counterexamples elucidate is politics. The acts of violence involved in terrorism arise from political motivation. Again, this is not yet enough and will have to be refined: many violent actions arise from a motivation to attain political ends—just wars, for example—yet we appear to be loath to call those terrorist. Before we can address that issue, though, this notion of a political motivation complicates matters.

Whether or not a particular violent act is considered terrorism most often seems to depend on one's political ideology or prejudice. Thus, most Israelis would consider Palestinian suicide bombings as terrorist acts, whereas a significant number of Palestinians and Arabs might characterize the same actions as freedom-fighting, acts of desperation, or attempts to overthrow an oppressive Israeli policy. And there are other examples of this, such as Chechen bombings in Moscow, the Tamil Tigers in Sri Lanka, the Contras in Nicaragua, and so on. Opponents paint these actors as terrorists and moral monsters, proponents as heroes and patriots.

What we are looking for, then, is a definition of terrorism that either shows it to be wrong in all cases or at least gives a description of activities similar to what we call terrorism that would be justifiable sometimes under particular and specifiable conditions.

Specialists in fighting terrorism operate under a particular definition of it in order to distinguish it from other kinds of behavior, usually criminal. For example, the Federal Bureau of Investigation defines terrorism this way:

> Terrorism is the unlawful use of force against persons or property to intimidate or coerce a government, the civilian population or any segment thereof, in furtherance of political or social objectives.

This definition is somewhat better than the ordinary usage one we looked at above, though there is a major difficulty with the notion of what may be unlawful. Taken strictly, this would mean that the acts of the French resistance in the Second World War as well as the assassination of Reinhard Heydrich (deputy chief of the Gestapo and "protector" of Bohemia and Moravia) by the Czech resistance would both be terrorist acts.

It could be that instead of "lawful" we should construe the force of the phrase to indicate "legitimate," though I do not think that will ultimately solve the problem. While our understanding of legitimate governments framing legitimate laws may be clear in some intuitive sense, it seems to evaporate once we try to apply it. Thus, while France and Czechoslovakia were clearly occupied countries in the Second World War, and thus the laws the Nazis passed regarding these two nations were illegitimate, the issue of legitimacy is much less clear regarding Chechnya, Palestine, and even the American colonies in the 1770s. In each of those cases, the issue of legitimacy is precisely what is being disputed. Nor does the self-determination of people provide very much help. In the case of the American Revolution, it seems that only one-third of the American population desired separation from Britain, the other two-thirds being split between Loyalists and those who didn't care either way. How to clarify and define legitimacy, then, just seems to sink us in another difficult problem.

Again on an intuitive level at least, the key and morally relevant feature that would distinguish terrorism from political assassination, for instance, regards who is targeted. So I think we will have fewer moral qualms about the killing of Heydrich—someone so cruel that even Nazis were frightened of him—than the blowing up of a schoolbus in an Israeli settlement.

Closest to expressing this moral intuition is a definition I have cobbled together from a variety of scholarly sources over the past ten years. As with most things in the academy, there is little consensus on the exact features of terrorism, but I am hopeful that at least in its main outline this is noncontroversial:

> Terrorism is the use of force for a political end involving the creation of terror or fear, seemingly random acts of violence, and the targeting of innocents or noncombatants.

I think this is considerably better than the FBI definition because it includes the latter's main provisions while eliminating the troublesome notion of unlawfulness. It also is superior because it adds two aspects that seem to be integral to the discussion of the immorality of terrorist acts—randomness and the targeting of innocents. The problem with this definition—and all definitions seem to have some problem—pertains more to a proper understanding of randomness.

It seems obvious that at least some of the targets of terrorists are not randomly chosen. Neither Yitzhak Rabin nor Aldo Moro were randomly chosen for assassination; and both the Murrah Building in Oklahoma City and the World Trade Center were specifically chosen. In fact, the World Trade Center was targeted twice. The World Trade Center was significant precisely because it served as a symbol for American dominance in international commerce. I think it is more likely that the pertinence of randomness is focused more on the victims than on the material targets themselves. If that is the case, then randomness should be linked more forcefully and clearly to the targeting claim: the targeting of random innocents or noncombatants is fundamentally what makes terrorism wrong. As Michael Walzer has written,

> Randomness is the crucial feature of terrorist activity. If one wishes fear to spread and intensify over time, it is not desirable to kill specific people identified in some particular way with a regime, a party, or a policy. Death must come by chance to individual Frenchmen, or Germans, to Irish Protestants, or Jews, simply because they are Frenchmen or Germans, Protestants or Jews, until they feel themselves fatally exposed and demand that their governments negotiate for their safety. (197)

I have the same problem with making noncombatantcy a morally relevant category for terrorism as I did in chapter 2; and I have the same objection to considering the civilian citizens of a nation as innocents, that is, as devoid of all moral responsibility for the activities of the state. It is therefore unnecessary for me to repeat those arguments. Elshtain, however, does raise a variant formulation that tries to focus on the relevancy of noncombatantcy:

> Terrorism is "the random murder of innocent people." The reference is not to moral innocence, for none among us are innocent in that way, but to our inability to defend ourselves from murderous attacks as we go to work, take a trip, shop or ride a bus. In other words, civilians are noncombatants. (18–19)

This formulation is exceedingly odd, because it stresses the victims' inability to defend themselves as the critical feature. Automatically, then, the bombing of the Marine barracks in Beirut, the attempted sinking of the *Cole,* and the attacks on the American embassies in Africa do not count as terrorist acts. In each of those cases the victims were either armed or guarded by soldiers bearing arms. In addition, none of the police officers killed in the World Trade Center would be victims of terrorism, because, having arms, they were able to defend themselves. Furthermore, it is not clear that, by this criterion, any violent act directed at civilians should be counted as terrorism. We in the United States have decided that the way we shall defend ourselves from attack is through the police function of the state for domestic threats, and the military for international threats. We are in that sense always being defended. In the case of the World Trade Center attacks, those defenses did not work. In other words, it wasn't that we were unable to defend ourselves against attack; it's that our defense mechanisms failed.

Elshtain continues in this vein:

> In a situation in which noncombatants are *deliberately* targeted and the murder of the maximum number of noncombatants is the *explicit* aim, using terms like "fighter" or "soldier" or "noble warrior" is not only beside the point but pernicious. Such language collapses the distance between those who plant bombs in cafes or those who fly civilian aircraft into office buildings and those who fight other combatants, taking the risks attendant upon military forms of fighting. There is a nihilistic edge to terrorism: it aims to destroy, most often in the service of wild and utopian goals that make no sense in the usual political ways. (19)

This passage may make for good rhetoric, but it does not bear up on even a cursory scrutiny. Elshtain's complaint is that terrorists do not take the risks that come from fighting other combatants. I assume she means the risk of death, since combatants are, by definition, armed and ready to kill. Yet not only did the nineteen terrorists who carried out the September 11 attacks face the risk of death, they embraced it as part of their mission. They also faced the risk of failure, one of the hijacked airliners not reaching its target. I am left to wonder what risks these terrorists did not face.

I am also left wondering what aspect makes terrorism nihilistic. Elshtain says that their goals make no sense in the usual political ways—but that is the point! The usual political ways do not appear to the terrorists to work, or perhaps usual politics does not address their goals. In these passages, Elshtain's objections to terrorism seem to amount to a considerable degree of frustration that terrorists do not engage in obviously futile endeavors: terrorists should attack only our well-armed and well-trained military and do so only after announcing their intentions so the military may be well prepared as well; and terrorists/all persons should promote and pursue only those goals that make sense in the context of the usual politics.

Terrorism is a tool of the desperate. It belongs to those who perceive gross injustice and oppression and who lack the political power to effect change through peaceful means. Their first order of business is to alter the political equation, and their tactics have not changed for well over a hundred years. As early as 1880, Narodnaya Volya, or the People's Will organization of tsarist Russia, published the aims of terrorism. This group, which served as a model for Lenin and the Bolsheviks, followed in a tradition of terrorism in Central and Eastern Europe. That tradition included the German radical Karl Heinzen, who wrote, in the revolutionary year of 1848, "If you have to blow up half a continent and pour out a sea of blood in order to destroy the party of the barbarians, have no scruple of conscience" (Laquer, 26). And in the late 1860s, Sergei Nechaev and Mikhail Bakunin each wrote a "catechism" for revolutionaries. The strategy that People's Will developed from these theorists encompassed four points:

[The aims of terrorist activity are to:]
1. Undermine the citizens' awe of governmental power.
2. Demonstrate the possibility of struggling against the government.
3. Lift the revolutionary spirit of the people and increase their faith in the success of the cause.
4. Organize forces capable of combat, that is, invite an escalating cycle of repression and response.

While the primary focus of terrorist attacks during this time was on governmental and business leaders, the basic principles hold true for contemporary attacks against civilian populations. The first two aims are directly linked. Terrorist theorists understand that the overwhelming power of the state need not be exercised continually for a population to be held in subjection. Power has a psychological as well as a physical aspect, and a population might well be held in check or subjugated through its awe—the intimidation and fear that arises from the might of the oppressor. In fact, it seems that the great colonial powers such as Britain relied more on this kind of intimidation than on the actual exercise of its military capabilities. It provides one explanation for the phenomenon of a century of British rule in India, which had then, as it does now, a much larger population than Britain. A terrorist act, therefore, begins to break the psychological effect of domination in that it shows that while the government may be powerful, it is also limited.

The second aim is closely related to the first. By showing that the government is not all-powerful and can be attacked, the terrorists show that armed struggle against the government is not futile. The more discord the terrorists can foment, the more they reinforce the notion that the subjugated population has a considerable amount of power to further their own aims.

If the first two aims are accomplished, the third will follow naturally. If the government is not as strong as the population had initially come to think, and if the people also have a significant amount of power themselves such that they can fight the government, then they will gradually become convinced that they can succeed in overthrowing the oppressor.

In many ways the final goal is the most interesting. Terrorists realize that even though very many people may be oppressed by a regime, the number of radicals that oppression will produce will be exceedingly limited. Revolutions are most often started by a small group of people who need to figure out how to mobilize the mass of citizens to the cause. Terrorists hope that their violent actions will provoke the state to be more violent and more repressive as a response. The more violent and repressive the state becomes, the more violence terrorists will inflict. In this spiraling escalation of violent responses, terrorists hope that governments will become so repressive that the mass of citizens will be mobilized to act and satisfy their overall goals.

Let me illustrate this point. Israel has a policy of destroying the houses of Palestinian terrorists who attack Israelis. I assume that the reasoning behind this policy is to exact a cost on the terrorist that extends beyond his own death or imprisonment. If his family is endangered with homelessness and the government demonstrates its willingness to exact that pain from his family, fewer terrorists will be willing to engage in hostile acts and may be deterred even if they would have killed themselves in the process of the terrorist act. It is likely, however, that this policy has the opposite effect. Since some of the Palestinian complaints point to Israel's alleged desire to drive Palestinians out of their homes in order to occupy more land, and that Israeli notions of fairness and justice do not apply to innocent Palestinians, the terrorist organizations gain huge propaganda advantages from these acts of retribution. Israel's policy appears to conform to and confirm the oppression the Palestinians experience. This, in turn, serves to radicalize and mobilize even more Palestinians to the terrorist cause and methodology.

Terrorism can flourish only if the group from which the terrorists spring and on whose behalf they act have serious and ongoing grievances against the target state. These are grievances that the group perceives as not being redressed or taken seriously. Terrorism is born from the hopelessness of the politically powerless and is sustained because it points a way toward power and hope, albeit through violence and death. Part of their argument maintains that targeted governments or states employ violence and death toward the oppressed group, so that must be the only language that the governments will understand. The members of the oppressed group who join terrorist organizations are then risking nothing, with the hope of gaining everything. Violent responses by states to terrorist activities may well satisfy feelings of revenge or answer the clamor for some kind of reaction, but they often play into the plans of the terrorist.

—————

Thus far I have been examining objections to terrorism that focus on terrorism's supposed violations of the principle of discrimination, condition (8) for *jus in bello*. Before completing that analysis, however, I would like to examine whether Islamicist terrorism satisfies the conditions for *jus ad bellum*, that is, whether those terrorists are conducting a just war. It seems appropriate to do this. Officials of the United States have often asserted that they consider the acts of September 11 to constitute acts of war, and the argument that terrorism is wrong because it violates condition (8) certainly also implies that terrorism is warfare. Walzer's claim that terrorism is not a form of warfare (197–98) seems to be silly in light of the foregoing. We must ask, then, what justification Osama bin Laden and Al Qaeda cite in defense of the steps they have taken.

As we have seen above, Elshtain describes Osama bin Laden's and Al Qaeda's motivation for engaging in terrorist acts against the United States as having two aspects. First, they desire to make the United States withdraw from world affairs into isolationism. Second, and of ultimate importance, they act the way they do because "they loathe us for who we are and what our society represents." By characterizing the aims of Al Qaeda and bin Laden in this way, Elshtain then argues that it is impossible for us to accommodate their views, and, more significantly, she Hitlerizes bin Laden and his movement. They are evil objectified and, like Hitler and the Nazis' attempted extermination of the Jews, they represent a mortal danger to America and, by extension, the West. Since the United States is facing an imminent and significant mortal threat to its political community, Elshtain has also made the case that America in particular and the world in general are confronting a supreme emergency that justifies the taking of extraordinary measures to defeat.

The issue becomes truly fascinating when one reads Osama bin Laden's "Letter to America" of November 24, 2002. In that document, written as a response to "What We're Fighting For"—a letter cosigned by both Elshtain and Walzer, among others, and issued on February 12, 2002—bin Laden engages in the same sort of Hitlerization as Elshtain does.

Bin Laden's is a very long letter in which he attempts to explain why he and Al Qaeda have targeted the United States. His complaints about the United States fall into three main categories. In the first, he claims that the American government has instituted and pursued policies that attack and oppress Muslims. He cites American military action in Somalia and Afghanistan as two examples of American soldiers directly killing Muslims but stresses throughout the letter that American support for Israel's treatment of Palestinians, for the Russians in their oppression of Chechnya, for India's activities in Kashmir, and for the Israeli incursion into Lebanon are indirect attacks by the United States against Muslims. In addition, bin Laden claims that American support of dictatorial rulers in Arab and Muslim nations also adds to the oppression of his people. He claims that Muslims have a moral as well as a religious obligation to overthrow these dictatorial rulers (perhaps as an expression of their right of self-determination), but that United States policy and economic and military support of those regimes make their task considerably harder if possible at all. In all of these cases, the supportive role of the United States in allowing and enabling various governments to oppress Muslim peoples is such a major factor that it is tantamount to the United States oppressing Muslims directly. Fighting against the oppressive regimes, then, entails fighting against the United States. In fact, bin Laden claims that if American policy and activities were to change, the material well-being and security of Muslims throughout the world would dramatically improve.

The second large category of objections that bin Laden raises in his bill of particulars is American economic oppression. Americans and American corporations are so fixated on profits that they will go to any length to secure them. Bin Laden claims that we are stealing oil from the Persian Gulf countries in particular, paying much less than the oil would be worth without our suppression of prices. He claims that the presence of American military bases in the holy land of Saudi Arabia and other Muslim countries constitutes a military occupation. This, conjoined with our support for repressive regimes, is done precisely to keep the oil flowing and prices artificially low. He argues that America is destroying nature with its industrial waste and that our refusal to sign the Kyoto Accord is to preserve the profitability of our corporations. In addition, he claims, "You are a nation that practices the trade of sex in all its forms, directly and indirectly." As such, we degrade women and denigrate basic human values in order to market our products. He maintains that we have used our power to destroy mankind "more than any other nation in history; not to defend principles and values but to hasten to secure your interests and profits."

The third category of accusations focuses primarily on American hypocrisy and godlessness. He claims that we operate according to a double standard regarding morals, principles, and values—one set for ourselves and one for others. We promote freedom and democracy for whites only, while for the rest of the world we "impose . . . monstrous destructive policies and governments." We do not respect United Nations resolutions and policies of international law, yet we selectively punish anyone else who fails to respect them. We censure war criminals and support international criminal courts to try them, but we demand immunity for our military personnel and government officials. While we claim to respect human rights, we use the same methods of the governments we censure for abuses: we have imprisoned thousands of Muslims and Arabs after September 11 "without warrant, trial or even disclosure of their names." We object to the way women are treated in Muslim countries, yet we exploit women like consumer products or advertising tools. We claim to be one of the most religious of nations, yet we separate religion from our politics and permit acts of immorality, considering them to be pillars of personal freedom.

When bin Laden puts forth what he wants the United States to do, it is clear that he is not demanding the kind of isolationism that Elshtain maintains he is. After calling on us to convert to Islam and leave Muslim countries—by which I believe he means withdraw our military installations—he wants us to stop our oppression of Muslims. This includes the acts of oppression we directly engage in as well as our political, military, and economic support of corrupt leaders in the Arab world. He also wishes us to curtail the aid we provide to the non-Muslim nations that oppress Muslims, such as Israel, India, Russia, and the Philippines. He wants us to take account of ourselves in order to recognize how our values are denigrated by our actions. Finally, he asks that America deal with and interact with Muslim people "on the basis of mutual interests and benefits rather than trying to subdue, steal from and occupy." Rather than withdraw, bin Laden is asking that we engage the Muslim world in a different way. In conclusion, as is very clear from his statement, bin Laden loathes us not for who we are but for what we have done and failed to live up to.

Clearly, through this process of Hitlerization, bin Laden is trying to utilize the same strategy as Elshtain: the United States is objectified evil. It is engaged in denying self-determination to Muslims and is ultimately responsible for the continuing global policy of the subjugation and murder of Muslims. According to him, on all fronts the Muslim community faces imminent threats to its survival: politically, economically, religiously, and culturally. This constitutes a supreme emergency for the entire Muslim people, so a war against the United States is justified, and those who fight the United States may take whatever steps are necessary to eliminate this threat to their survival. As Michael Walzer has written:

> We might better say that it is possible to live in a world where individuals are sometimes murdered, but a world where entire peoples are enslaved or massacred is literally unbearable. For the survival and freedom of political communities—whose members share a way of life, developed by their ancestors, to be passed on to their children—are the highest values of international society. (254)

Bin Laden provides an account of collective responsibility similar to the one I argue flows from the logic of war in order to justify the killing of civilians by his terrorist acts. The American people have chosen their government and agree to its policies—that is the basis of their choice; therefore, the American people have chosen to consent to and affirm the oppressive policies and actions listed above. The American people bear the ultimate responsibility for the actions of their government that do not discriminate between combatants from noncombatants. "If we are attacked we have the right to attack back."

Yet, even without resort to this account of collective responsibility, we have already seen how supreme emergencies can sanction whatever means are necessary to eliminate threats, from the curtailment or suppression of basic human rights to the direct and intentional killing of civilians.

———

It is not my intention to be an apologist for Al Qaeda or to provide support for the actions of Osama bin Laden. But if Elshtain's analysis of his motivations is the dominant view in the United States, as I believe it is, then we are not being truthful. Bin Laden's complaints—hyperbolic as some of them might be—are not novel. Our allies and many others in the international community have leveled similar charges against us for decades, and even a cursory examination of our history in many parts of the world, especially Latin America, gives considerable credence to his views. The American government and American people have been and continue to be curiously blind to the cumulative effect our policy decisions have on other people around the world, especially on those who lack political power or economic clout. We are rightfully proud of the good that we have done, but we do not seem to care about the harm. If we wish to defeat the violence around us, the first step would be to engage the truth: we should be as quick to acknowledge the accuracy of the complaints against us as we are to point out how they are erroneous.

Nor was it my intention to give advice on foreign policy to the United States government. My intent over these pages was to show that just war theory and the doctrine of supreme emergencies cut both ways. If just war theory and supreme emergencies—especially as used by Walzer and Elshtain—are sufficient to sanction the killing and destruction inherent in conventional and total wars, then they are sufficient to sanction terrorism as well: to accept one as right and proper is to accept the other, and this means we have no moral basis to object to what Al Qaeda and other terrorist organizations are doing. The United States responds to an attack that was, in itself, a response to an attack; the attempt of one to eliminate a threat to survival constitutes a further threat to survival for the other; and since each party to the conflict is evil objectified, all communication and negotiation are appeasement. The only alternative either side has is to violence, which begets more violence, until one or the other or both are destroyed.

Even on secular terms, this is immoral and pathological. How any Christian could reconcile this reasoning and the actions that follow from it with the call to live a life of discipleship to Christ is something I cannot comprehend.

Fifth Meditation

Matthew 7:21–27

It is not anyone who says to me, "Lord, Lord" who will enter the kingdom of heaven, but the person who does the will of my Father in heaven. When the day comes many will say to me, "Lord, Lord, did we not prophesy in your name, drive out demons in your name, work many miracles in your name?" Then I shall tell them to their faces: I have never known you; *away from me, all evil doers.*

Therefore, everyone who listens to these words of mine and acts on them will be like a sensible man who built his house on rock. Rain came down, floods rose, gales blew and hurled themselves against that house, and it did not fall: it was founded on rock. But everyone who listens to these words of mine and does not act on them will be like a stupid man who built his house on sand. Rain came down, floods rose, gales blew and struck that house, and it fell; and what a fall it had!

■ Lord, help me to remember that I am always in your presence.

I am glad, Lord, finally to have a straightforward meditation, this passage coming right after your Sermon on the Mount. And it seems to be apt, since I have been talking in the previous chapters about evil and evildoers. But there are problems in what you say.

I do wonder, though just a little bit, why the prophet, the exorcist, and the miracle worker are not known by you. I am about to talk about Dietrich Bonhoeffer and he seems to fit at least one of those categories, so I need to be clear. It seems that the prophet, exorcist, and miracle worker are all doing the will of the Father, and they are acting in your name, so I am not sure why

99

you call them evildoers. As a matter of fact, they do not appear to be doing evil at all, but rather a great deal of good. So, are they doing good but not following enough of the will of the Father? Seems that something must be missing from what they are doing, but I'm not sure what that could be. It is as though you are saying that not following all of what you've taught us is the same as doing evil, but that is too severe a standard, isn't it? It seems that inadequacy or omission would be one thing, but actually doing evil by doing an incomplete good—if that is what you mean—is difficult for me to understand.

All right, so it turns out not to be so straightforward. Let me try it again. I arrived at the idea that what the prophet, exorcist, and miracle worker were doing was incomplete because it appears that they were doing *some* of what you taught. They must have asked for the gifts in your name, and the benefit of what they do is given to your people—because you don't mention that they are acting out of pride or for their own self-aggrandizement. But all of that is insufficient. Now, it seems that it isn't insufficient for service, for you yourself did all three of those actions during your time walking with us. So it clearly must be insufficient for salvation.

I have written in this book about my problems with the power your child Augustine attributes to internal dispositions: how internal dispositions and intentions can alter what an action is. Augustine seems to say that an internal disposition or intention can make an action incomplete, that we can exclude certain kinds of effects. That makes no sense to me. And in this passage, I think you may be talking about incomplete internal dispositions.

I am thinking about all of this because I have moved to the second paragraph in this reading. Both the sensible man and the stupid one have built houses that, I guess, are very similar, perhaps so much so that they are indistinguishable. But the problem with the latter's house is the weak foundation. The sensible man's house is strong because he listened to you and acted on it, whereas the stupid man listened and did not act on it. What are the houses supposed to be? They are clearly metaphors, but what do they stand for?

Initially, I thought the house was the action, and the foundation was the listening to the word, but that doesn't fit what you say. I must be making a distinction you do not admit, because it seems you are talking about two different things: the first is listening to/acting on the words, and the second is listening to/not acting on the words. The listening part only appears to be the same. And maybe the building of the houses only appears to be the same also.

Here's what I think you mean. The houses may look identical to each other, but in reality each house and its foundation is a distinct unit. So even though stupid's and sensible's houses appear to be the same, they are very different, and only sensible's will stand the tests. Then the prophet, exorcist, and miracle worker might at first appear to be your disciples because they show all the signs disciples should display, but if their foundations are not rooted firmly in your word, then, even if they are successful for a time, what they build will not last.

The other thing that occurs to me is that we do not normally have access to the foundation. That is known to you alone. Yes, I am trying to escape Paul in that last Meditation. Because you are focusing on acting upon what is heard, all of us should know it, judge it, and toss the evildoer out. So what's the difference between these two passages, or have I merely repeated what I already should have learned?

I am guessing that the difference is that Paul seems to be targeting hypocrisy, and this passage from Matthew is targeting incompleteness. It isn't that the stupid are hypocrites; it's that they do not take it far enough. The stupid seem to truly believe in your word, they desire to live in your house, but they do an incompetent and clumsy job of it. They perform the grand gestures, what everyone can see, but I guess you are saying they are not doing it all. Our lives in you must include what no one sees; what everyone talks about is the least important to you.

No. There I go dividing what you make whole. The grand gesture—the prophecy, exorcisms, and miracle-working—will come as they come, through you. The praise is yours. Our listening to your word and acting on it means that you will know us, will recognize to whom we belong. So that's it? Listening to all you say and acting on it all unites us with you, and the mere listening and not acting unites us with . . . I'm not sure what that unites us with.

Is it uniting us with the world, with other persons instead of you? You do not point to Satan in this passage, and the only thing I see is that the evildoers are helping others. This remains a problem for me, so it seems I am not understanding this passage well. Your Sermon does require us to help others, to love others. Is there a way that we love others that precludes our loving you, or a way of serving others that is not consonant with the will of the Father? If that's right, then maybe you are telling me that the good I do must be out of love of you, and the love of others flows only from that. The love of you is the foundation upon which I should build the house of loving others. I've often heard it said that it is important for Christians to be children of God and not humanitarians. Even if what we do looks like what humanitarians do, what it is that we are doing—following you—is different.

Reading this, I sound more sure than I feel.

Bless my mind to illuminate me with your wisdom;
bless my lips to allow me to speak your word;
and bless my heart that I might live the gospel.

5

The Men behind
the Hitler Question

Prologue

Helena worked for many years as a switchboard operator and receptionist for a small firm in the Bronx. She had a slight German accent and seemed to be an older woman when I first met her in 1977; I guessed she was on the sunny side of sixty-five, nearing retirement or supplementing a retirement income by answering phones in a little cubicle off the front door. I met her when I went to her firm to interview for a job. We spent a lot of time together that day, because the person I was supposed to interview with never showed, leaving me sitting in a hard folding chair in Helena's cubicle. She impressed me, though, both by her friendliness and by the amount of coffee she drank and the number of cigarettes she smoked. I think we were barely visible behind the clouds of smoke in her cubicle, and we earned a few looks as we argued loudly about opera, the relative merits of Donizetti and Puccini.

I didn't get the job, but I kept coming by occasionally to see Helena, bringing coffee and a bialy for breakfast, and an extra pack of cigarettes. She gave me an excuse to get out of bed during those days of unemployment, and her boss either didn't mind or was frightened of her tongue. For an hour or so we'd laugh and try to provoke each other by insulting operas or performers or authors we found the other liked.

That year for my birthday some friends had chipped in and bought me two tickets for a Saturday matinee performance of Turandot at the Metropolitan Opera. I wasn't dating, and none of those friends would be caught dead going to the opera—even for something as mainstream as Turandot—so I thought I would ask Helena. Though I knew she loved Puccini, I was a bit reluctant because I also knew she was Jewish and wasn't sure if she was observant. I didn't want to tempt her by having to decide between Shabbat and opera, a choice I would have found easy to make; nonetheless, I still had something of a conscience.

It wasn't a problem. She hadn't been to services, not even High Holy Days, for years. She did, however, have another appointment earlier in the day up in Yonkers and didn't think she would be able to make it in time for curtain. She seemed to be reluctant to talk about it, but I felt comfortable enough to ask if I could give her a lift. Neither of us had a car, but I knew someone who would lend me his. After she refused a lot and I insisted a lot, she finally agreed that I could pick her up and we would go to breakfast before her meeting.

The Saturday came and I pulled up to her apartment building. She was waiting on the stoop but didn't wave back. I stepped out of the car, figuring she hadn't seen me, but she had. She wouldn't get in. I tried to make a joke about driving slowly and safely, but her expression told me she wasn't in a joking mood. She wouldn't look at me and said she would take the train.

I had no idea what was wrong. I parked the car and ran after her, trying to find out what the matter was. At some point she turned and looked at me. She rolled up one of her sleeves and showed me a tattoo. She was a survivor of Belsen, a Nazi concentration camp. She would not ride in a Volkswagen, not even one driven by me, not even if she would miss her appointment. She would not get in, and I could not, would not argue with her.

After a silent train trip, we were only a few minutes late for the meeting in Yonkers. She was one of three survivors talking to a church group about what it was like to be in the camps. I found out she was just a little over fifty; her accent thickened and she was not animated when she spoke; there was a dullness in her eyes.

We missed Turandot. We sat in a coffee shop near her apartment, smoking cigarettes and drinking coffee, not saying anything. When we walked to her building, I told her I didn't understand. She said that no one did.

Within a year she emigrated to Israel.

———※———

■ Up to now we have spent a considerable amount of time examining and critiquing just war theory. What I have hoped to show in the preceding chapters is that just war theory is untenable. Among other things, just war theory contradicts itself in that it sanctions the killing of innocents, which it at the same time prohibits. In addition, just war theory can also be used effectively to justify all wars. Even if we accept the killing of innocents as justifiable in times of supreme emergencies—a contention that is, at best, highly problematic—the notion of supreme emergency is so flexible that very many cases seem to satisfy its criteria. Indeed, in my examination of Elshtain's application of Walzer's theory, I think it is clear that the justification of war sanctions even the gross barbarism of Osama bin Laden and Al Qaeda, as well as terrorism in general.

All of the preceding chapters, even if they are successful in what I intended them to do, are still nothing but philosophy. I do not mean to put philosophy down or denigrate the work that philosophers do. Some of us have done interesting and valuable work in our attempts to understand thought, explain concepts, and clarify experience. Yet philosophy, even when it is done well, is something of a bloodless enterprise in that it is so abstract and apparently removed or distanced from lives as people actually live them. In many ways, this is the source of philosophy's beauty, appeal, and value: it gives us the tools and opportunity to pull ourselves back and think about the bigger picture.

So I do not mean "nothing but philosophy" to be a bad thing entirely, but especially when one is contemplating evil and war, I think philosophy needs to open its arms a bit more widely and embrace some flesh and blood. It is an important thing for us to consider the nature of evil; it is even more important that when we consider the nature of evil that we also see the ovens of Auschwitz and the killing fields of Cambodia. If we do not, then we run the risk that "understanding" evil will become solely an exercise in reading definitions in Merriam-Webster. Likewise, I may speak and argue about the untenability of war as a response to evil, but we need to wonder whether these objections have any reality when a real person comes face to face with real evil—smells its breath, if you will. So in this chapter I want to spend some time examining some people of recent history and contemplate their roles in what we have been considering. This will still be philosophical—remember the zebra and her spots—but also more concrete.

At this point in each of the many outlines I constructed before beginning to write this book, I intended to talk about Hitler. As I sat down to actually put pen to paper, though, it occurred to me that there really wasn't a whole lot to say about the man. There has been plenty said about Hitler already, so I am not sure what it is that I can add or emphasize that we all didn't know or realize before.

We know Hitler, after all. He is probably as familiar to us as most of our presidents. Perhaps more so as I think about the likes of Rutherford B. Hayes and Benjamin Harrison. As I write this, Amazon.com offers over 32,000 books about Hitler, and I would be willing to wager that sometime very soon after I write this there will be another significant biography of him published by a major historian or author, as well as several significant academic studies produced by university presses. And this is just counting the market in the United States.

Hitler sells. When I mentioned the title of this book to a colleague—not even bringing up what it is about, since that seems to be a real conversation stopper—he told me that it was a good idea, because people love buying books about Hitler, especially if I put a picture of him in uniform and a swastika on the cover.

My colleague is right, and the questions that flow from his being right are at least two: why are we so fascinated by Hitler? And does that evident fascination have anything to do with the Hitler question? Hitler has obviously assumed a level of significance for us that is very curious. For those of us in the West—for I am not sure that Hitler betokens the same phenomenal fascination across cultures—Hitler has come to signify the highest (or lowest) of evil. He is the embodiment of hatred, murder, death, and destruction. In so many ways we are the children of the Enlightenment and have come to value and esteem the power of rationality and reasoned discourse, especially in politics and our other social interactions. For the most part our culture has dispensed with the image of Satan as a real being that used to serve the role of embodied evil for our forebears before the seventeenth century. Perhaps for all of our rationality and methodological scientific inquiry, there is some need that we have to personify evil, to give it not only a name but a face and a personal history. Perhaps this makes the phenomenon of evil less abstract.

I am a philosopher and, either by training or by nature, I love the abstract much more than the concrete particular. But it appears that for most normal people, the more abstract an idea is, the less reality it possesses. The reality of evil, then, would need to be made less abstract so that we all can see how real and how dangerous it truly is. By specifying a key example of the utmost evil, we can come to recognize another manifestation of it more easily and be on guard against it better than we would be otherwise.

Even if we assume that little bit of social psychology is correct, I still think it is curious that we take Hitler as the figure and symbol for the embodiment of the utmost evil. Consider that, at least in terms of sheer numbers of innocents intentionally and directly slaughtered, Josef Stalin's record of murders supersedes Hitler's. Stalin ruled the Soviet Union for about thirty years, compared to Hitler's twelve in Germany. During that time he initiated pogroms and purges, eliminated the Kulaks as a class, used starvation as a weapon, engaged in antisemitic persecutions, and maintained a constant state of terror for the populations under his control until some tens of millions were left dead.

So, Stalin appears to be more bloodthirsty than Hitler. Indeed, he could be the greatest monster of the twentieth century, sprinkled liberally as it is with tyrants, dictators, and states that carried out systematic murders, genocides, and terror campaigns. Given the stature of a Stalin, why is it that Hitler is the one who provides the standard by which we measure evil and analogize the worst behavior of leaders and states? Amazon lists almost half as many books about Stalin as about Hitler; why is it that there have been so many more biographies and studies of Hitler than of Stalin? Why is so much of our curiosity and fascination centered on the one rather than the other?

It can't be the horror. Let me rephrase that. It can't be the horror alone that makes Hitler the paradigm of evil that fascinates us so much that we keep coming back to examine and reexamine him and his life. We do not try to understand Stalin or Pol Pot to anywhere near the same extent that we do Hitler. We are content to write them off, comparatively speaking; they drift to the edges of our consciousness where they dwell with Franco, Tojo, Pinochet, and Mao: their histories are more prosaic instances of cruelty. So if it isn't the scale of the horror or the extent of the terror, what is it that attracts us to Hitler? What is it about his particular repellency that draws us to him so that all evil is characterized under his name?

In one very early draft of this chapter I wrote that I thought we find Hitler so fascinating because he appears to us to be so much a normal human being. Perhaps it is easy to relegate Stalin to the second tier of cruel dictators because Stalin seems to lack precisely those features Hitler seems to possess in abundance, and through which he was able to seduce the German *volk*. It is interesting to note that Hitler was a seducer: from the way he was able to deliver a speech and capture both the fears and aspirations of the German people, to the way he managed the development of the cult of his personality, to the way he seduces our attention so many years after his death. Some people I know joke that the History Channel on cable should be called the "Hitler Channel."

I recall the first time I saw film footage of Hitler in some television documentary about World War II. He was down on one knee, smiling and joking with a very pretty, pigtailed, blonde little girl of seven or eight. It was a genuflection before Aryan youth. And that screen image was soon followed by another one showing him cavorting and playing with a couple of dogs on the balcony of his house in Berchtesgaden. The impression I took away and still retain was exactly the one intended by the original propagandist if not by the documentary's editor, namely, Hitler's fundamental humanity. He seemed to be so much like the people I like—the older men in my neighborhood while I was growing up—and the thought that he was also and at the same time such an evil person that he defined *evil* did not quite fit. For a long time I thought it was this discontinuity between the grandfatherly figure, playing with children and dogs, and the author of the Final Solution that is what I found fascinating.

That basic humanity was a feature that Josef Stalin lacked. As far as I know, Stalin was never known as a great orator, not even as good as Trotsky. Nor does his personality seem in any way dynamic, even as a younger man. He strikes me more as Mr. Salerno did in my old neighborhood: a shopkeeper whose smile wasn't convincing, his face just a mechanism used to watch and make sure that I didn't steal any peaches. Stalin looked like a middle-level bureaucrat and appeared awkward during his obligatory pictures with pigtailed Soviet girls, who looked, by the way, just like their Nazi counterparts.

But as I reflected on it, the fascination we have with Hitler is not explained by some aspect of his attractiveness or appearances of his benevolence. All seducers must appear attractive on some level—or be attractive in some way—just to have the opportunity to seduce their victims. Over fifty years ago Simone de Beauvoir wrote about the continuing fascination with another evil person who was also a noteworthy seducer. About the Marquis de Sade she pointed out, "The fact is that it is neither as author nor as sexual pervert that Sade compels our attention; it is by virtue of the relationships which he created between these two aspects of himself" (12).

Perhaps much the same applies to Hitler. We are not simply fascinated—that is my first mistake. He compels our attention. And he compels our attention not as a brutalizing, murdering monster, nor as the child- and dog-loving man who would be a secular messiah, but as the particular combination of the two. Further, there is another relationship created between those aspects of himself and the position he held as leader of his people. To apply a trite and well-worn notion, Hitler compels our attention because we recognize so much of ourselves in that web of relationships.

The recognition that is spoken of in this notion is a commonplace, psychological answer, and it is inadequate insofar as we limit its scope to Hitler's personality, character, and history and try to analogize them to our own personal stories. Different people are always similar enough to one another that parallels and analogies are rather easy to make. Even so, I am sure there are some nontrivial similarities between Hitler and any one of us—myself, for example—such that I could derive some insights into my own phobias and neuroses by comparing myself to him. Nonetheless, it is not so much the psychology of Hitler that compels our attention as it is the political psychology he represents: how Hitler's vision and person expressed, captured, and seduced the vision of the Western world. He compels our attention in a way that Sade and Stalin do not precisely because of the politics. He seduced the people of Germany to the point of their self-destruction and seduces the people of Europe and the rest of the West to the point of their moral degradation. Even de Beauvoir would have to admit that seeing the seducer alone is to see nothing; we must also see and consider the seduced.

There is a certain attractiveness to this elaborated view of de Beauvoir's account. Some major part of its attractiveness is that it flatters us into seeing ourselves first and primarily as scholars studying the relations between phenomena: we are social scientists or literary critics, which amount to the same thing these days. Further, we are rescued from too much positivism and objectivity by the connections we make from the phenomena we are studying to ourselves. If we simply take the complex of Germany of the 1920s through the 1940s, analyze the data, graph them, and perform some statistical processes on them, then we can understand it and, naturally, apply the results to ourselves and our own situation. It is something like combining Einstein's researches into relativity with Freud's personal practice of self-analysis. Understanding the complex relational phenomenon that is Hitler gives us power over it, and that power, once we possess it, will keep us safe from a repetition of it in the future.

Of course, most of us are not social scientists, let alone Einsteins, and not even social scientists or Einstein are social scientists or Einstein all of the time. Perhaps there is also a rather large element of voyeurism in our fascination with Hitler. I think it might be akin to the way so many of us tend to slow down and rubberneck at bad automobile accidents on the expressway. We want to see the ugliness and destruction of the mangled cars as well as what blood there might be, and oftentimes this desire seems to be almost against our wills. We are fascinated with the crash. Its invitation to us to look is overwhelmingly compelling, perhaps especially since we are driving similar cars on the same roadways under the same conditions. There is a great deal of sympathy, I'm sure, that arises within the drivers as they pass the scene, but also I'm sure that there is some measure of self-congratulation: it really is too bad that fellow is not me with my greater skill, or kinder fortune, or superior foresight not to have another drink with dinner. Perhaps, then, we look upon Germany under Hitler as a particularly horrible traffic accident, and as we look, we experience it with a fusion of a sense of pity for all those who have been harmed and a sense of pleasure or satisfaction at the pain we have avoided by our greater character or our finer societal virtues and values.

There is another kind of understanding operative in this kind of voyeurism as well. In the case of the social scientist, there is an understanding of the material, sociological, and psychological factors that formed the preconditions for the Holocaust and an application of them to the present. This second kind of voyeuristic understanding also recognizes the similarities between our condition and the condition of Germany or Europe, and we recognize it well enough to raise a frisson of fear, but it also and simultaneously confirms our faith in ourselves and in our own ultimate safety. We continue to drive after passing the wreck, more slowly than before and maybe more attentively, but safely and securely. I sometimes imagine that most of us come to think that we would react to the rise of Nazi power with some variation on the von Trapp family: one step ahead of the Gestapo, escaping over the mountains to Switzerland and on to the resumption of an innocent life of four-part harmony in a Vermont ski resort.

The trouble is that Hitler and the Holocaust are not understandable. We can examine the German economy after Versailles and the ineffectuality of the Weimar government as well as the history of German and Central European antisemitism fed by the Christian churches over millennia, and it simply does not add up. We can look at the banality of the evil as Hannah Arendt's work expressed it, and explore how the bourgeoisie cooperated with the Nazi regime in order to maintain their social and financial security, and that doesn't add up either. The evil of Hitler and the Holocaust does not make any sense. When Germany faced a labor shortage after 1943, they still killed the Jews, enslaving relatively few. When railcars and rolling stock could have been used to ferry needed munitions and medical supplies to the front to help the armies defend the nation, they were commandeered instead to transport more Jews to the death camps. Germany's defeat and destruction were hastened by the

Final Solution. And instead of bringing greater safety and security to the bourgeoisie, the Holocaust brought degradation and death to them—all of which was foreseeable. For Stalin and the other dictators, there was some kind of pragmatic logic at work behind their killings. In the European Holocaust there appears to be none.

Not even the analogy to the car accident ultimately works. With car accidents we may not know the precise cause, but the list of possible causes is small: icy road conditions, speeding, faulty brakes, driving under the influence. . . . But we don't know the cause of the evil of Germany under Hitler, so we cannot understand it or approach understanding it. Hitler fascinates not because he was evil but because we don't understand him or the phenomenon he represents. It is the fascination of mystery, with no Dick Francis to tie up the loose ends of the story. Hitler is the bogeyman under the bed we know is there, even though his being there makes no sense. He draws our attention in the same way the Loch Ness monster and Jack the Ripper do, except that, unlike with the bogeyman, Nessie, and the Ripper, about whom we know so little, the more we come to know about Hitler, the less the mystery and our curiosity and our fears diminish. With more examination, the mystery, curiosity, and fear increase.

Hitler, therefore, has become a symbol for all those threats to us that appear immune to rational discourse, pragmatic calculation and bargaining, and appeals to self-interest or moral goodness. There is no way to engage the threats Hitler represents according to any of the rules of civilized behavior. The evil that Hitler represents is simultaneously beyond our normal experience of life and social interactions and yet also a part of the air we breathe every day. Not far from the surface, we are a fearful people. We are afraid of terrorism and confused by the immunity the terrorists display toward rationality, negotiation, and compromise. We are fearful of literally senseless murders and the random harm that seem to flourish in our cities and follow us to the suburbs. We are fearful and anxious because evil seems to be omnipresent, lurking next to us and our loved ones—the evil that threatens, defies understanding, and remains beyond our control.

This is why I began this book with the claim that pacifism or peacemaking or whatever pietistic pie-in-the-sky label I may use for nonviolence is absurd. This is also why my comments about Christians and warfare that I made at the end of the last chapter were rather more rhetorical than heartfelt. The kind of nonviolent response to evil and Hitler that I advocate is foolishness because it will not be heard, nor will it be effective. It is so likely that evil will triumph in the face of pacifism that it would be irresponsible, dangerous, and downright stupid to pursue it. This is also why showing the philosophical inconsistencies behind just war theory is inconsequential; and any exercise that even comes close to making a moral equivocation between the United States and Al Qaeda or terrorists appears inane. Both attempts strike us as pedantic nonsense barely of interest to academics. The issue is not political philosophy or theological politics, but rather survival in the face of an implacable, fanatical foe bent on our destruction. The death we face is not a theoretical one.

I want to turn, then, to something a bit more specific, namely, an examination of how pacifists have actually engaged evil. For this section I will talk about two of the most famous pacifists of the last century: Gandhi and Dietrich Bonhoeffer.

Mohandas Gandhi

I think it is fair to claim that Mohandas Gandhi is one of the primary patron saints of pacifists. He and his methods served as a model for many, not least of whom were Martin Luther King Jr. and much of the American civil rights movement. He is hailed as a person who steadfastly maintained his commitment to peace during his confrontation with significant political opposition and oppression.

About a year after Gandhi's assassination in 1948, George Orwell wrote an essay entitled "Reflections on Gandhi," which was partly a book review of Gandhi's newly published autobiography but was also much more a critical examination of Gandhi's life and methods. Orwell began the essay with a curious sentence: "Saints should always be judged guilty until they are proved innocent, but the tests that have to be applied to them are not, of course, the same in all cases" (328). In the body of the essay, Orwell puts Gandhi's sainthood to the test.

Orwell was not impressed with Gandhi. He found Gandhi's homespun clothing, vegetarianism, and emphasis on religion unappealing, and he thought Gandhi's plan for India was "medievalist" and "obviously not viable in a backward, starving, overpopulated country." Orwell gets most interesting when he turns to Gandhi's pacifism—his program of *satyagraha*—by which he and his followers engage in nonviolent resistance to British rule in order to gain independence for India, a project that was ultimately successful. Orwell's take on Gandhi's pacifistic resistance strikes a fascinating note:

> It was also apparent that the British were making use of him [Gandhi]. Strictly speaking, as a Nationalist, he was an enemy, but since in every crisis he would exert himself to prevent violence—which, from the British point of view,

meant preventing any effective action whatever—he could be regarded as "our man." In private this was sometimes cynically admitted. The attitude of the Indian millionaires was similar. Gandhi called upon them to repent, and naturally they preferred him to the Socialists and the Communists who, given the chance, would actually take their money away. How reliable such calculations are in the long run is doubtful . . . but at any rate the gentleness with which he was nearly always handled was due partly to the feeling that he was useful. (329)

What Orwell is pointing out in this passage is that Gandhi was permitted to engage in his nonviolent program of resistance because of the general feeling on the part of both the British authorities and wealthy Indians—two of Gandhi's targets—that his movement was preferable to other kinds. From the British perspective, Gandhi helped preserve civil peace; from the perspective of the wealthy, Gandhi co-opted the message of the leftist reformers and other radical political movements. But each of these powerful opponents agreed that Gandhi's movement could and should be tolerated because it was ineffectual and permitted the continuation of the status quo with a minimum of disruption. In fact, the disruptions caused by general strikes and periodic boycotts served as a pressure valve whereby Indian nationalists could be convinced that they were doing something significant to advance their cause when in actuality they represented merely an inconvenience to the powers of the colonial administration. It is, therefore, not the case—as some have asserted—that the British in India were gentle imperialists. While it may be true that British colonial rule was more benevolent than the Belgian or the French, for example, the British apparently treated Gandhi gently because they perceived his value in sustaining their rule.

Orwell also reports that Gandhi himself was posed with a variation of the Hitler question in 1938. His response is worth noting:

In relation to the late war [World War II], one question that every pacifist has a clear obligation to answer was: "What about the Jews? Are you prepared to see them exterminated? If not, how do you propose to save them without reverting to war?" . . . Gandhi's view was that the German Jews ought to commit collective suicide, which "would have aroused the world and the people of Germany to Hitler's violence." After the war he justified himself: the Jews had been killed anyway, and might as well have died significantly. . . . If you are not prepared to take life, you must be prepared for lives to be lost in some other way. When, in 1942, he urged non-violent resistance against a Japanese invasion, he was ready to admit that it might cost several million deaths. (333)

Orwell opines that Gandhi did not understand the nature of totalitarian regimes and considered that all conflicts were relevantly similar to his struggles against the British colonial government:

> The important point here is not so much that the British treated him forbearingly as that he was always able to command publicity. As can be seen from the phrase quoted above, he believed in "arousing the world," which is only possible if the world gets a chance to hear what you are doing. It is difficult to see how Gandhi's methods could be applied in a country where opponents of the regime disappear in the middle of the night and are never heard of again. Without a free press and the right of assembly, it is impossible not merely to appeal to outside opinion, but to bring a mass movement into being, or even to make your intentions known to your adversary. (333–34)

Orwell presents formidable obstacles. Totalitarian regimes target the leadership of the opposition first, so that a mass movement against the regime can be throttled in the cradle. Without access to the press or other means of publicity, even with a leadership intact, it is very hard to see how the mass of people necessary for Gandhi-like resistance can ever get started, since the means of coordinating action nationwide among a huge number of citizens are absent. But Orwell does not stop at these objections.

> But let it be granted that non-violent resistance can be effective against one's own government or an occupying power: even so, how does one put it into practice internationally? . . . Applied to foreign politics, pacifism either stops being pacifist or becomes appeasement. (334)

Orwell not only questions Gandhi's assumption that the Jews of Germany could engage in collective resistance against the Nazi regime and arouse world opinion against Hitler's policies—an assumption that rests on the further, dubious assumption that Orwell does not point out: that the world at large would care about the fate of the Jews of Europe if only it knew of their suffering, a position that I am not so sure was true, given what the Western powers did know about the oppression of Jews in the 1930s and 1940s. But Orwell also skewers the notion that pacifism can be an effective tool in international relations. If world public opinion were aroused against the Nazi treatment of Jews, what would follow if those nations were committed to nonviolence? Orwell's answer is that the world would be faced with only two choices: remain nonviolent and let the deaths continue, or dispense with pacifism and engage the Nazi regime militarily. There is no third option.

Finally, Orwell underscores the most basic premise underlying Gandhi's resistance through nonviolence: all human beings have a conscience that can be appealed to, and that conscience will respond to generosity and peaceful gestures. Orwell points out that this presumption is not necessarily true when one is engaged with the insane, and not only can we question Hitler's sanity—since his hatred for the Jews appears to be the height of irrationality if not insanity—but we can also question the sanity of a German culture that fostered and supported Nazi antisemitism. In order for nonviolent resistance to be effective, we must be dealing with precisely the kind of perpetrators Hitler and his followers were not. They needed to have some measure of goodness within them that could be called out. But, by definition, they were the epitome of evil, so nonviolence would accomplish nothing but more death and evil's ultimate triumph.

Dietrich Bonhoeffer

Throughout Orwell's essay on Gandhi, the notion of sainthood runs as a leitmotif; and though Orwell argues—successfully, I think—that it is possible to separate Gandhi's pacifism from his religion to some extent, it is ultimately what Orwell has to say about Gandhi's sainthood that gives the bite to his critique of nonviolence:

> Of late years it has been the fashion to talk about Gandhi as though he were not only sympathetic to the Western left-wing movement, but were integrally part of it. Anarchists and pacifists, in particular, have claimed him for their own, noticing that he was opposed to centralism and State violence and ignoring the other-worldly, anti-humanist tendency of his doctrines. But one should, I think, realize that Gandhi's teachings cannot be squared with the belief that Man is the measure of all things and that our job is to make life worth living on this earth, which is the only earth we have. (331)

According to Orwell, Gandhi's sainthood was essentially antihuman, since it flowed from a notion that either one could serve God, and therefore do what is right and avoid sin in the doing, or one could value this world and become chained to all the attachments that would keep one from God. Orwell focuses on Gandhi's rejection of close friendship to make his point clear.

> Close friendships, Gandhi says, are dangerous because "friends react on one another" and through loyalty to a friend one can be led into wrong-doing. This is unquestionably true. Moreover, if one is to love God, or to love humanity as a

whole, one cannot give one's preference to any individual person. This is again true, and it marks the point at which the humanistic and the religious attitudes cease to be reconcilable. To an ordinary human being, love means nothing if it does not mean loving some people more than others.... The essence of being human is that one [unlike Gandhi] does not seek perfection. That one *is* sometimes willing to commit sins for the sake of loyalty, that one does not push asceticism to the point where it makes friendly intercourse impossible, and that one is prepared in the end to be defeated and broken up by life, which is the inevitable price of fastening one's love upon other human individuals. No doubt alcohol, tobacco, and so forth, are things that a saint must avoid, but sainthood is also a thing that human beings must avoid. (331–32)

In this one long paragraph that I have quoted from, Orwell encapsulates the problem much more clearly than I could. By his understanding, Gandhi's religious belief—and most probably religious belief in general—precludes humanism and loyalty to one's friends: to be a saint is to be inhuman, and to be human is to reject sainthood. From the perspective of the saint who pursues perfection, the demands of loyalty to one's friends ineluctably require one to commit sins. Here at last we have a most succinct statement of Walzer's position—that even though the killing of innocents in a supreme emergency is wrong, one must do it anyway: it is a sin one must commit if one is fully human. For those of us who are religious and do not aspire to sainthood, our lives consist of dynamic tensions between what our humanity mandates and what our faith requires, and it is a tension that, under certain circumstances, will demand resolution one way or the other.

I have begun this section of the chapter on Dietrich Bonhoeffer with Orwell's reflection on Gandhi's sainthood because it offers something of a template for my understanding of Bonhoeffer's life. Many acclaim Bonhoeffer as a saint (see Slane 2004, for example), and if Eberhard Bethge's largely hagiographic biography of Bonhoeffer were sufficient to convince me that he was a saint, he would be a saint more in the mold of a Joan of Arc than a Francis of Assisi: more warrior than peacemaker. Nonetheless, Bonhoeffer has a significant appeal not only to Christian just warriors like Elshtain but also to Christian pacifists like Stanley Hauerwas. Neither Bethge nor the just warriors nor the pacifists have ever come close enough to reconciling the tension that is apparent in Bonhoeffer's life, or to explaining how the divergences of his thoughts and actions unite in some kind of sympathetic consistency or interplay, or whether one trend of his theology is rejected for the sake of another.

I am speaking, of course, of the compatibility of Bonhoeffer's advocacy of Christian pacifism that he wrote about so clearly and eloquently in *The Cost of Discipleship* (more recently translated as *Discipleship*) with his joining in the conspiracy to assassinate Hitler.

In *The Cost of Discipleship,* Bonhoeffer focuses the central portion of his argument on an exposition of the Sermon on the Mount and maintains that the primary aspects of being followers of Jesus—what *discipleship* means, in other words—are contained within his call and promise. Much is encompassed within these middle chapters, as well as the book as a whole, which deserve study, reflection, and prayer; and while I am loath to pull out only small sections and, thus, decontextualize them, I think it is necessary to give some elaboration of what Bonhoeffer took to be entailed by following the way of Christ.

He writes:

> *"Blessed are the peacemakers: for they shall be called the children of God."* The followers of Jesus have been called to peace. When he called them they found their peace, for he is their peace. But now they are told that they must not only *have* peace but *make* it. And to that end they renounce all violence and tumult. In the cause of Christ nothing is to be gained by such methods. His kingdom is one of peace, and the mutual greeting of his flock is a greeting of peace. His disciples keep the peace by choosing to endure suffering themselves rather than inflict it on others. They maintain fellowship where others would break it off. They renounce all self-assertion, and quietly suffer in the face of hatred and wrong. In so doing they overcome evil with good and establish the peace of God in the midst of a world of war and hate. But nowhere will that peace be more manifest than where they meet the wicked in peace and are ready to suffer at their hands. The peacemakers will carry the cross with their Lord, for it was on the cross that peace was made. (126–27)

For Bonhoeffer, the renunciation of violence is not a good to be pursued in itself; he is making explicit what is implied by becoming a disciple and living as Christ lived. Christians intend to live as Christians, and insofar as we are faithful to the gospel, evil will be overcome by good; if we maintain fellowship in Christ with all persons, the peace of God will follow. But at all times our focus should be on living a life of faithfulness. Faithfulness in following Jesus means that Christians renounce every personal right they possess for his sake (156), including revenge and personal retribution. What follows from this is patient endurance:

> The right way to requite evil, according to Jesus, is not to resist it.

This saying of Christ removes the Church from the sphere of politics and law. The Church is not to be a national community like the old Israel, but a community of believers without political or national ties.... [The Church] has abandoned political and national status, and therefore it must patiently endure aggression. Otherwise evil will be heaped upon evil. Only thus can fellowship be established and maintained. (157)

In this passage, Bonhoeffer clearly indicates that the church is something separate from national states. As we have seen in earlier chapters, the primary function of the state is the defense of citizen rights from both external attacks from other, aggressor states and also from internal, criminal threats. Since Christians renounce their rights by following Christ, clearly there is nothing for the state to defend. Allegiance to Jesus replaces national allegiances, and the claims of Jesus negate the claims of states, in the same way that the requirements of citizenship negate the requirements of discipleship. Loyalty to one is incompatible with loyalty to the other. Fellowship is maintained only by living the life of faith, and nothing must interfere with that, especially our personal rights. Christians, therefore, are always "other" in the nations; we are aliens, a people set apart.

At this point it becomes evident that when a Christian meets with injustice, he no longer clings to his rights and defends them at all costs. He is absolutely free from possessions and bound to Christ alone.... The only way to overcome evil is to let it run itself to a standstill because it does not find the resistance it is looking for. Resistance merely creates further evil and adds fuel to the flames. But when evil meets no opposition and encounters no obstacle but only patient endurance, its sting is drawn, and at last it meets an opponent which is more than its match. (157–58)

Injustice and evil seek resistance as a means to perpetuate themselves and become stronger. Violence breaks the bonds of fellowship—even as only a response to violence—and is contrary to the gospel precisely because violence flows from a valuation of things: material property, rights, even the love of life itself. Rather than maintaining these kinds of things, the Christian is called away from them and toward being bound to Christ and living faithfully. Evil is beyond our power to resist; we can only encourage it by ourselves.

To leave everything behind at the call of Christ is to be content with him alone, and to follow only him. By his willing renouncing of self-defense, the Christian offers his absolute adherence to Jesus, and his freedom from the tyranny of his own ego. The exclusiveness of this adherence is the only power which can overcome evil. (158)

The renunciation of self-defense—by most accounts the most basic of basic human rights—is entailed by the Christian's exclusive love and valuation of Jesus. Bonhoeffer expresses this as a freedom from the tyranny of the self, which subordinates all other things when threatened. In so doing, he gives affirmation to Orwell's claim that religious faith is antithetical to the belief that man is the measure of all things and further supports the fundamental opposition of the humanistic and the religious. Bonhoeffer professes that God is the measure of all things and following Christ is subordinate and subservient to nothing else.

> We are concerned not with evil in the abstract, but with the evil *person*. Jesus bluntly calls the evil person evil. If I am assailed, I am not to condone or justify aggression. Patient endurance of evil does not mean a recognition of its rights. . . . The shameful assault, the deed of violence and the act of exploitation are still evil. The disciple must realize this and bear witness to it as Jesus did, just because this is the only way evil can be met and overcome. . . . Suffering willingly endured is stronger than evil, it spells death to evil. There is no deed on earth so outrageous as to justify a different attitude. The worse the evil, the readier must the Christian be to suffer; he must let the evil person fall into Jesus' hands. (158–59)

Bonhoeffer is trying to concretize his discussion by moving it from the realm of an abstract theological discourse on evil to the everyday world where we encounter evil persons. In this passage he is stressing the requirement that Christians have of speaking the truth, of calling evil by name and bearing witness to it. This aspect of Bonhoeffer's work and its implications for the Christian community is discussed wonderfully in Stanley Hauerwas's *Performing the Faith*. It is not for Christians to suffer in silence, to acquiesce to the evil person's deed, but to proclaim the evil person's evilness and, in so doing, witness to Jesus. By doing all of this, the Christian allows the evildoer to pass into Jesus's hands—the ultimate act of faithful renunciation. Only Jesus can overcome the evil; only Jesus can heal and transform the evildoer.

As I hope is obvious to anyone who may read this book, I agree completely with the view expressed in *The Cost of Discipleship*. I think it is also obvious that that agreement makes the following questions crucially important: What happened to Dietrich Bonhoeffer? Why did Bonhoeffer move from this understanding of the gospel, which is so clear and so uncompromising, to the position of a conspirator against Hitler, even to the point where Bonhoeffer was willing to kill Hitler himself?

Bonhoeffer did not leave any record of his transformation. This is hardly surprising, since he spent the last few years of his life in Nazi custody; one would not expect him to leave any incriminating evidence that would further endanger his life, the lives of his friends, or the lives of others involved in the conspiracy. But the absence of a record leaves a haunting gap in our understanding of this man's faith journey. We do have two sources of information about Bonhoeffer during those days: his friend Eberhard Bethge, and the fragments he wrote from his cell, published posthumously as *Letters and Papers from Prison*. In the "Editor's Preface" to *Letters and Papers*, Bethge writes:

> Through [Bonhoeffer's] brother-in-law Hans von Dohnanyi [who also would be killed by the Nazis] he was given a glimpse behind the scenes of the crisis that centered on General von Fritsch, and of the plans for overthrowing the Nazi government that were associated with General Beck. Up till then Bonhoeffer, under American and English influences, had been very near to absolute pacifism—a virtually unheard-of position in Germany at that time. Now he began to see pacifism as an illegitimate escape, especially if it tempted him to withdraw from his increasing contacts with the responsible political and military leaders of the resistance to Hitler. He no longer saw any way of escape into some region of piety. (xix)

In this passage Bethge admits that Bonhoeffer was "very near to absolute pacifism"—a characterization that he studiously avoids in his biography of Bonhoeffer—but he seems to minimize it as an effect of outside influences and as outré for German intellectuals at that time (indeed!). Bethge intimates that by the time Bonhoeffer returned to Germany from travel abroad and joined the Abwehr (the German military intelligence service) and the conspiracy, he was coming to regard Christian pacifism as irresponsible and entailing a withdrawal into pietism. Bethge implies that Bonhoeffer came to reject what he advocated in *The Cost of Discipleship*, if not in all cases of evil apparently triumphing, then at least in the extreme case of Hitler's Germany. One could conclude, then, that Bonhoeffer came to accept some form of just war theory based on this reasoning.

This would make some sense as a solution for the dilemma of Bonhoeffer's transformation. If he was not committed deeply to peacemaking as entailed by discipleship—if it was a temporary aberration in his theology, in other words—his reversion to a more standard theology that makes room for warfare under certain, constrained circumstances (like Walzer's supreme emergencies) seems to make his theological vision more consistent.

I am not convinced this is the best answer. Bonhoeffer was aware to a large extent of the evil Hitler represented before he wrote *The Cost of Discipleship*. Not only were Hitler's speeches and writings clear about his aims, but the Nazi press was continually publishing tracts of hate; in April 1933 a national boycott of Jewish businesses was declared; in September 1935 the government promulgated the first of the notoriously oppressive Nuremberg laws; and in November of 1938 the Krystalnacht pogrom—state-sponsored and state-supported—resulted in mass destruction of Jewish property as well as the rapes and deaths of hundreds. Further, Bethge reports that during this time Bonhoeffer himself was searching for ways to resist Hitler's regime. In short, I do not think Bonhoeffer received any information regarding the evilness of the National Socialist government that made him change his mind and join the Abwehr and conspiracy in 1940 that he did not have or foresee when he published *The Cost of Discipleship* in 1937.

But what makes Bethge's analysis most implausible is contained in a letter Bonhoeffer wrote on July 21, 1944. The date is significant because it is the day *after* the unsuccessful attempt to assassinate Hitler, and it is clear that Bonhoeffer had learned of the failed attempt while imprisoned. He wrote:

> I thought I could acquire faith by trying to live a holy life, or something like it. I suppose I wrote the *Cost of Discipleship* as the end of that path. Today I can see the dangers of that book, though I still stand by what I wrote. (193)

Bonhoeffer did not abjure the views he expressed in 1937 even after the choices he made in the intervening years and despite the hopes he had that Hitler would be killed. Rather, he recognized the dangers in what he advocated in *Discipleship*. Still, he maintained that he had gotten it right. The implication that Bonhoeffer saw the error of his Anglo-American-influenced pacifistic ways does not quite fit well enough with all the evidence: he conspired to kill Hitler and even offered to do the job, while at the same time he stood by the peacemaking doctrine of *Discipleship*.

There is another answer, which harks back, yet again, to Walzer's discussion of supreme emergencies. In *Embodying Forgiveness*, L. Gregory Jones suggests an approach to this Bonhoeffer dilemma that is significantly different than Bethge's. Noting that for Bonhoeffer repentance demands action, Jones writes:

Bonhoeffer recognized, particularly though not exclusively in his struggle against the Nazis, that it is difficult to discuss precisely how Christians ought to embody practices of forgiveness and repentance in specific social and political circumstances. Such discernment involves the work of the Holy Spirit, particularly as the Spirit guides Christian communities in their practices. . . . Perhaps because of the absence of such Christian community, Bonhoeffer concluded that there are times of "extraordinary necessity"—like the predicament posed by Nazi Germany—in which it is unclear what ought, or even can, be done to resist the encroaching darkness. In such situations, the "ultimate question remains open and must be kept open, for in either case man becomes guilty and in either case he can live only by the grace of God and by forgiveness." (27; the quotations are from Bonhoeffer)

With this approach we can see that it is probable that Bonhoeffer considered himself faced with a choice between two terrible options. Knowing that he must act, but not knowing how to act, Bonhoeffer considers each of his only alternatives to be unsatisfactory: whichever one he chooses will result in guilt. For the purposes of our discussion, then, it seems that Bonhoeffer considers nonviolence, peacemaking, and the patient endurance of suffering to be an inadequate response to the extraordinary circumstances of the evil of Hitler. Surely, responsible action demands that one do what is necessary to eliminate the threat that appears triumphant. On the other hand, the gospel seems to demand peacemaking and the renunciation of violence as part and parcel of what it means to follow Christ. Thus, no matter which avenue he pursued, Bonhoeffer considered that he would not be acting faithfully. Jones continues:

Even when "responsible action" is justified by "necessity," however, Bonhoeffer contended that the Christian is not freed from his or her relation to and need for God's forgiveness: "Before other men the man of free responsibility is justified by necessity; before himself he is acquitted by his conscience; but before God he hopes only for mercy." The person "hopes" for God's mercy; he or she cannot presume it. If it becomes a presumption rather than something that must be hoped and prayed for under the reality of God's judgment, then the action loses its quality of repentance and becomes a cheap and venal grace. This is how Bonhoeffer understood his own involvement in the resistance and in the plot to assassinate Hitler. (27)

I think Jones gets Bonhoeffer's thinking right, but I also think Bonhoeffer struggled with this conclusion considerably. He appears to wrestle with it in a passage from *Letters and Papers from Prison* that, before reading Jones, I had considerable difficulty understanding:

> Although it is certainly not true that success justifies an evil deed and shady means, it is impossible to regard success as something that is ethically quite neutral. . . . In the last resort success makes history; and the ruler of history repeatedly brings good out of evil over the heads of the history-makers. Simply to ignore the ethical significance of success is a short circuit created by dogmatists who think unhistorically and irresponsibly; and it is good for us sometimes to grapple with the ethical problem of success. As long as goodness is successful, we can avoid the luxury of regarding it as having no ethical significance; it is when success is achieved by evil means that the problem arises. In the face of such a situation we find that it cannot be adequately dealt with, either by theoretical arm-chair criticism, which means a refusal to face the facts, or by opportunism, which means giving up the struggle and surrendering to success. (5–6)

In this passage Bonhoeffer switches his focus to outcomes as a way to explore the dilemma and apparently ends with equivocation. That the death of Hitler and the end of the Nazi regime would be a good result no one denies, yet that good result is insufficient to justify the evil of violence against him. Nonetheless, that good result is not something a responsible Christian can simply ignore. If the result is truly good, and if the only way to achieve it is through evil means, it is foolish for Christians not to grapple with the dilemma, because it is an inescapable one. Bonhoeffer goes on to say that it is not possible for us to escape our responsibility for the course that history takes, for it is a responsibility that has been laid upon us by God.

Bonhoeffer equivocates because he does not justify violence by extraordinary necessity: he does not maintain that his intention to participate in the killing of Hitler was a good thing—he asserts precisely the opposite: that it was evil. On the other hand, he does not justify Christian pacifism either, because it implies a renunciation of responsibility for the evil situation persisting unchecked and a "refusal to face the facts." Neither option is good, and all that is left for the Christian is to struggle, make the most faith-filled decision possible, and trust in the merciful forgiveness of God.

Finally, though, Bonhoeffer did not equivocate: he made his choice, and that choice to enter into the conspiracy remains a significant one, even though he apparently does not justify it.

I think I recognize something of the enormous crisis and struggle that Bonhoeffer endured in the last years of his life, and it is not for me—living this comfortable life—to second-guess him, devalue that struggle, or accuse him of bad faith. In many ways I agree that Bonhoeffer is an exemplar of Christian life. Even with all that said, however, I think he erred in how he understood the dilemma. It is not clear to me that God has laid responsibility on us for the course that history will take; Bonhoeffer himself alludes to the power of the ruler of history and how he wields it over the heads of the history-makers. But if we were responsible for history, Bonhoeffer's dilemma would shake my faith much more deeply. As unsatisfactory and philosophically untenable as I found Walzer's discussion that performing evil actions is inescapable when confronting supreme emergencies, that intellectual dissatisfaction pales in significance when I consider Bonhoeffer's parallel conclusion that there are situations in which I have no alternative but to sin.

As is obvious from the meditations I am sharing in this book, I am often confused by God's Word and reluctant to follow the way of Christ even when I fully understand what he means. Yet even considering my own willfulness and limitations, I cannot bring myself to believe that there are situations in which being faithful means that I *must* sin.

This is not simply my own predilection; it is not that I *prefer* not to be placed in situations where I must sin. The doctrine, rather, is simply not comprehensible, because it is contradictory. As Christians it is our most fundamental belief that Jesus is Lord and came to save us from sin and death. If following Jesus leads us to no alternative but to sin, then our faith is a mockery. If all sin is, as I believe, basically derivative from the first sin—Adam and Eve's arrogant desire to be like God (Gen. 3:5)—discipleship and faithfully living the Word cannot lead to it. When we are confronted with situations that seem to leave us no alternative but to sin and do that which is evil in the sight of God, then it is clear that *we* are misunderstanding something, not that God requires us to do something which he forbids.

This is why I have to consider that Bonhoeffer was wrong in the way he understood the Hitler question.

Sixth Meditation

1 Corinthians 1:18–29

The message of the cross is folly for those who are on the way to ruin, but for those of us who are on the road to salvation it is the power of God. As scripture says: *I am going to destroy the wisdom of the wise and bring to nothing the understanding of they who understand. Where are the philosophers? Where are the experts?* And where are the debaters of this age? Do you not see how God has shown up human wisdom as folly? Since in the wisdom of God the world was unable to recognise God through wisdom, it was God's own pleasure to save believers through the folly of the gospel. While the Jews demand miracles and the Greeks look for wisdom, we are preaching a crucified Christ: to the Jews an obstacle they cannot get over, to the gentiles foolishness, but to those who have been called, whether they are Jews or Greeks, a Christ who is both the power of God and the wisdom of God. God's folly is wiser than human wisdom, and God's weakness is stronger than human strength. Consider, brothers, how you were called; not many of you are wise by human standards, not many influential, not many from noble families. No, God chose those who by human standards are fools to shame the wise; he chose those who by human standards are weak to shame the strong, those who by human standards are common and contemptible—indeed those who count for nothing—to reduce to nothing all those that do count for something, so that no human being might feel boastful before God.

■ Lord, help me to remember that I am always in your presence.

In answer to the question, "Where are the philosophers?" Lord, one of them is right here. As I check back to Isaiah 19 where Paul takes this reference, I see that the preceding verse reads, "Pharaoh's wisest councillors make up a stupid council."

Excuse me. I am dodging this reading by checking the references outlined in the text of my Bible. I am afraid I do take pride in my intelligence, and I prize rationality whenever I achieve it in my thoughts or see it in the work of others. I don't know that I am wise, though I often confuse intelligence with wisdom, but I wish to be. I have always regarded my intelligence and rationality as a gift from you so that I might work better and, more important, might understand how I should be and what I should do. This passage throws me into confusion yet again and on an aspect of myself that I would usually trust more than others. So much so that I don't know where to begin or what to pray upon once I do start.

When Paul says it was your own pleasure to save believers through the folly of the gospel, I think some of my trouble with you began to make sense, in a backward kind of way. All of these years I have told you in a variety of ways that I am confused or that I don't understand what you want from me, sometimes in the tone of a bratty teenager. And here you are letting me know that I should be confused and I should not understand. I don't even know how to analogize it. It's like we are both speaking English, but our words don't mean the same thing to us—the same language but different meanings.

What I have done through most of my life is try to understand, and what I have ended up with are obstacles and foolishness. I am Jewish in that I ask you for miracles, for the signs that you are truly there, that you'll take care of me, that you are who scripture says you are; if only you would do something unmistakably like a god would do, I could believe with some assurance that I am not kidding myself with a comfortable mirage or Freudian delusion. I am Greek in that I study your Word and the words of the saints looking for wisdom—something that would make sense of my life, my success and failures, and my death that I know will come too soon no matter how late.

Well, let me play to what, before now, was my strength. I remember an insight from a German philosopher or theologian (why do you make the best ones always Germans?) who wrote that when God became human, humanity became divine. There is more than a hint of pride in that statement, but still it is too general or abstract for us now. There is a way in which I do consider myself divine when I pray and consider your Word: what I have tried to do is understand the gospel by making it fit into my experience and conform to my rationality. Your Word needed to become understandable to me in order for me to believe it and live it. Very subtly, so that I don't realize that it's happening, I make myself God, and you have to prove yourself to me and satisfy my requirements. As a result, your Word is both obstacle and foolishness, maybe because you won't play this game.

The crucified Christ is a folly. Right off the bat I have to admit that I don't see that. I confess my belief and try to get my belief to conform to my mind and experience so that it can work for me, so that it can make sense with everything else that I think is true about myself and your people. On my worst days, I make the gospel conform to what I want to do and how I want to be, citing "proof texts" and the "real" meanings behind the words and the stories. The problem, Lord, is that I don't think I am aware of doing that. I see my desires and my needs or the pain of others and make you answerable for them—demanding either your miraculous intervention or else the wisdom to understand. When you provide neither in ways that I can see them, I call you to account and my faith is shaken.

I know that I have to invert all of this: rather than making your Word conform to my mind and experience, I need to conform my mind and experience to the gospel. Instead of evaluating you by my standards and what passes for my wisdom, I must evaluate myself by your standards and your wisdom. That much is obvious. What is not so clear is what your standards are. I don't know how it helps me to know I must listen to the fools; I don't even know how the fools and the weak shame me. I am reduced to nothing by those who are common and contemptible, but I am so out of touch that those words strike me as just words. I do not feel reduced; I do not feel as though I am nothing. In my own eyes I remain a god.

I do what you ask and consider how I have been called, and I am left with a blank. I don't remember being called as an event or as something that happened to me on a particular date or at all. I know that you have called and are calling me, but I can't locate it. I do recall and can locate calling you and asking you to follow me. And I do also recall turning around and seeing that you are somewhere else. As usual, I chase after you as though you are some wayward child and ask you again to follow me. Perhaps in this gentle and annoying way of yours, you are getting me to follow you, even though what I am thinking is that you are periodically distracted: you lead me where you will even as I try to carry you away. And I can't help but wonder now if the only way I can understand you is through the miracles I ask for and expect but never see. Must everything be a paradox?

Bless my mind to illuminate me with your wisdom.
Bless my lips to allow me to speak your word.
And bless my heart that I might live the gospel.

6

Success, Failure, and Hypocrisy

■ I tried to show in the last chapter that Dietrich Bonhoeffer focused on the importance of responsible action in time of necessity and that for him, responsible action ultimately meant taking up arms against Hitler. In the last quotation I cited from *Letters and Papers from Prison,* Bonhoeffer speaks of the impossibility of regarding success neutrally, as something that is ethically insignificant; and he further contrasts dogmatists—the armchair critics who refuse to face the facts—with the opportunists who surrender to success. He apparently concludes that one must consider the value of success but not use the good result as a justification of evil means: that those who pursue success in times of necessity had best pray for God's forgiveness.

Throughout the essay from *Letters and Papers* in which that passage appears, Bonhoeffer speaks a great deal about responsible action, and as the circumstances of his life indicate, he concluded that responsible action included conspiring to kill Hitler and end the madness of the Third Reich. I am left to wonder why Bonhoeffer considered violence a responsible action and how he ultimately regarded the pacifism he espoused in *The Cost of Discipleship.* Pacifism in the face of the evil that was Hitler appears to be irresponsible, perhaps either because it entails inaction or because the action it involves is inadequate to secure success. Maybe the two amount to the same thing in the end.

George Orwell again offers some clear thinking and useful insight on this question. In 1942 there was a fascinating exchange published in *Partisan Review* between Orwell and three English pacifists. Having the last word in the exchange, Orwell justifies his contention that

> Pacifism is objectively pro-Fascist. This is elementary common sense. If you hamper the war effort of one side you automatically help that of the other. Nor is there any real way of remaining outside such a war as the present one. In practice, "he that is not with me is against me." The idea that you can somehow remain aloof from and superior to the struggle, while living on food which British sailors have to risk their lives to bring you, is a bourgeois illusion bred of money and security. . . .
>
> I am not interested in pacifism as a "moral phenomenon." If Mr. Savage [D. S. Savage, a poet and pacifist] and others imagine that one can somehow "overcome" the German army by lying on one's back, let them go on imagining it, but let them also wonder occasionally whether this is not an illusion due to security, too much money and a simple ignorance of the way things actually happen. . . . Despotic governments can stand "moral force" till the cows come home; what they fear is physical force. (226–27)

This is language that is very similar to Bonhoeffer's description of the armchair dogmatists who refuse to face the facts. What both Bonhoeffer and Orwell are pointing to is the bourgeois illusion that a pacifist—either Christian or secular—can withdraw from the conflict; that one's refusal to engage in violence is an attitude born of moral superiority, above and beyond the cretins who wage war; and that from this aloof standpoint, one can examine the issues with a dispassionate regard for the political issues and actors. For these pacifists, war is an intellectual problem that they have solved for themselves. One of the things that bothers Orwell the most, though, is that the insularity pacifists assume is false. As he points out, the refusal to fight fascism is tantamount to aiding it; to remain aloof is to support the war effort that Hitler and the Germans are making. Insofar as pacifist propaganda and arguments have any effect on the war, they cannot but help one side at the expense of the other: if the pacifists were to convince the British people to follow their example, Hitler would defeat his enemies and achieve his war aims.

What is most illuminating is the insight Orwell offers that the kind of pacifism espoused in England in 1942 was bred by security. Pacifists may remain sanguine and aloof from the conflict precisely because their safety is being assured by others who are willing to engage in violence—to kill and be killed. Because the Allied armed forces are not aloof or insulated from the conflict it is possible for the pacifists to retain the illusion that they are superior to and separate from the war and to have nothing to do with either side, who are each equally wrong. This is the stance of the hypocrite who, from his position of safety and comfort, both decries the source of all the benefits he enjoys and feels entitled to and maintains an attitude of moral superiority to those who provide for him.

Comfort tends to make us blind. We do not ask where the bounty comes from, assuming it is ours by right and cannot be taken away. Comfort makes us insensitive to those who are victims. There is an unreality to pain and suffering and death because we perceive them to be so distinct from us that we are immune to them; that we can stand apart because we are apart. It is a tautology, but true nonetheless: safety makes us secure. But that security is, as Orwell points out, a bourgeois illusion. Because I am safe and well fed and have a good job, so can others be safe, well fed, and employed if only they work harder and aren't so stubborn. Since I am nonviolent and can be persuaded by rational argument, so at base is everyone, and warfare is simply a foolishness born of a pessimistic attitude.

The Hitlers of the world encourage such an attitude, as much now as in 1942. As Orwell points out, tyrants and conquerors are immune to moral suasion and rational arguments; "what they fear is physical force." The same force that they find successful is what they worry will be successful against them. If Bonhoeffer is right—that in the last resort success is what makes history—then the significance of being successful is the determination of what history will be, which is also, therefore, the determination of the future. With that in the balance, necessity would demand whatever means to achieve success, especially if the only alternative is illusion and a refusal to face facts as they are, not as we would wish them to be. And may God forgive our opportunism.

This, then, is the problem with pacifism as Orwell and, I believe, Bonhoeffer see it. Pacifism entails withdrawal and the assumption of insularity. By refusing to engage in violence, the pacifist ultimately helps the cause of evil; pacifism is hypocritical, because pacifists enjoy the fruit of violence in the defense of their security; and, finally, pacifism as a strategy to combat evil is ineffectual and doomed to be unsuccessful.

I think the problem, though, is really much worse than this.

Some of the difficulties I have had in thinking about pacifism as well as trying to write about it as part of what it means to be a disciple of Christ stem from an oversimplified view of it. Too often it seems that the primary concern of both Christian and secular pacifists has been dictated solely by the way states resolve international disputes when diplomacy fails. It is natural enough for those of us who call ourselves pacifists to focus on war, because it has been and remains so prevalent and destructive an option. Defense budgets grow enormously even during times of quiescence—if there are any quiescent times anymore—so that it appears that nations are either actively engaged in war or are preparing for the next one because of ever imminent threats to survival or ways of life. I read somewhere that in the contemporary world Clausewitz's dictum has been turned on its head: politics is the extension of warfare by other means. War and the threat of war have been prevalent throughout the fifty years of my life, and as Thomas Hobbes pointed out, war and the threat of war amount to the same thing: a condition of mind and spirit that is prepared to receive or to do violence. If that's the criterion for a state of war to exist, then it is hard for me to think of or imagine a time when humanity was at peace.

As pacifists, our focus on inter-nation warfare is incomplete. Peacemaking should be more appropriately concerned with the phenomenon of violence, of which warfare conducted by the armies of nation states is only a part. We need to focus much more on that condition of mind and spirit that is prepared for violence, because it is that condition that provides the ultimate ground for warfare and leaves us amenable to both its justification and its necessity, as well as, I think, to its inevitability. If our minds and spirits are so conditioned that violence is natural and fundamental to human nature, then there can be no vision of or aspiration to an alternative way of being.

Thinking about violence rather than warfare centers our attention more appropriately where it should be, because violence pervades not only our environment but our experience and our character as well. We can understand why a resort to warfare seems so self-evidently justified, why warfare appears to be normal, and why pacifism stands in need of justification. While warfare is what states do, violence is what we do, and that violence provides a template for many of our ordinary interactions. Violence is so pervasive and determining that it seems close to impossible to eliminate it or even to countenance its elimination. As a dear friend is fond of saying, "What do you expect from a pig but a grunt?"

While it is clearly true that violence is expressed in the clash of armies on battlefields and the bombs and bullets of air forces and terrorists, violence also characterizes all relations involving domination, even though some domination may not result in bloodshed or death. Violence exists in the exploitation of workers by their employers, in the verbal abuse of one spouse by the other. It exists even in political campaigns where candidates or their surrogates misrepresent and are misrepresented, are vilified and

exalted. We can see violence in our schools, not only by the physical attacks in hallways but in the presence of firearms and knives in backpacks
and the fear that leads to students carrying weapons, and in the fear that
installs metal detectors in doorways. We see it in the extremes exhibited
by teachers: both domination and neglect are illustrative of a violent attitude. There is violence in the financial and stock markets and in the
currency exchanges. There is violence in the pollution spread by industry,
agriculture, and motor vehicles; violence in ecological protests; violence
in pornography and the way the sexes view each other.

Even though the list can go on, I can already hear the objections: "It
is precisely this kind of extremist view that makes your pacifist position
ludicrous and intellectually untenable." I can also hear my more patient
critics explain that I have almost certainly overstated the case. While it is
possible that violence would be an apt descriptor for, perhaps, some of the
relations I point to, it does not seem at all appropriate for others on the
list, or for my implication that violence is the predominating characteristic
of most of our relations to one another and our interactions. That latter
claim, especially, is at best hyperbolic and, at worst, a function of an overly
ideological imagination.

So, I believe I owe my patient critic a little bit more. Emmanuel Levinas
spurred my reflection above when he wrote,

> Violence is to be found in any action in which one acts as if one were alone
> to act: as if the rest of the universe were there only to *receive* the action;
> violence is consequently also any action which we endure without at every
> point collaborating in it. (6)

Violence, as Levinas points out, is the expression of the solitary person
and is inescapable for the solitary person. That is not quite the most explicit statement of his point, though. Violence does not just arise from the
solitary—for to tease out a feature Levinas only alludes to, if one were in
fact alone, it is not clear that the violence that would be expressed would be
of much concern. It is not simply the solitariness that needs to be emphasized but more that the solitary sees and considers herself to be the most
important being in the universe, or considers herself to be the universe
itself. Whatever concerns her or may be in her interest is what ought to
concern all or is in everyone else's interest, if anyone else's interest matters
at all. Her desires become paramount, and everyone else has a duty to
satisfy them. Her safety is most important, and all else has an obligation

to secure it. Her understanding of the world is the truth to which all else must conform.

Violence is the expression of the arrogance of selfhood. It displays itself in all relations where the self is primary, or in Levinas's terms, the self is solitary. Levinas says "*as if* one were alone to act," which indicates that none of us ever is primary or solitary, but there seems to be a point at which our continual "as ifs" blind us to what is real—what the facts are that we refuse to face. Levinas is right to focus on the centrality of "as if alone," but that must also be conjoined with a sense of superiority as well as an ability to act. Ultimately, violence comes from power, the ability to act the way one wills. If I can act as if I were alone to act upon the universe, I have the power of God and I am God. That is the sin of violence.

When one is solitary, superior, and powerful, one is not only God but, more importantly, immune. I don't think we try to become God simply to be God but rather because if I were God, then nothing could harm me. In the language of contemporary philosophy and theology, solitary superiority and power are the mechanisms by which one becomes the ultimate Subject and all else is Other. *Alone* means "all one." The Other cannot reach this ultimate Subject except on the Subject's terms: contact, friendship, fellowship, and love occur only if the Subject allows, and they grow only so far as the Subject wills. Violence is born of the egotist with power.

Having said that, the problem is that, to a greater or lesser extent, we are all egotists and we all have power. This is where the second half of Levinas's description comes in: "any action which we endure without at every point collaborating in it." We are not solitaries. We are social and enmeshed in a web of interpersonal relationships. We desire the immunity of God precisely because we are acted upon by others continually, and we seem never to collaborate at *every* point. As much as we perpetrate violence, we suffer it at least as much. What does collaboration with an action mean ultimately but to will it for myself? And it also seems clear that if I were able to collaborate with the act at each and every point and, by so doing, will it, the action would be *my* act; I would in fact be acting through another, which is the height of power. If the action is the expression of someone else's will, it seems impossible for me to will it also, simultaneously. At some point I must acquiesce before I can reach the point where I can will it for myself—and this refers only to actions that I welcome!

It should be clear that I am asserting something odd if not counterintuitive: even beneficial actions are also violent unless they were collaborated in at every point. Goodness can victimize us. I think immediately of performing a kindness for someone only to be met with his anger rather than

134

his gratitude. I remember those instances so well because of the resentment that grew in me because the gratitude was owed and not paid. In some cases at least, my favors may be acts of violence if they are gifts of my superiority bestowed from my generosity. I am victimized by goodness when the favor done for me underscores my vulnerability and neediness. When we do not "cooperate" and will the action for ourselves, we experience the action as violent because it is a diminution or deprivation of our superiority as well as an intrusion upon our aloneness by an Other whom we cannot stop or control. Violence is visited upon the egotist without power.

I am surely not saying that violence characterizes all of our relationships all of the time. I am not even sure that this kind of view predominates in all of our interactions. But I am also sure that we are, and are tempted to be, egotists much of the time and that we will tend to moderate it only under certain circumstances. Insofar as this captures us, we are both omnipotent and powerless, perpetrator and victim.

Furthermore, I think this provides a handy template for international relations. To some extent I believe that nationalism and patriotism, especially the way we have been experiencing them in the United States recently, are describable as a transference of our individual egotism to the collective itself, that is, the state. We ascribe the highest value to democratically discerned self-determination and see the willingness of all to follow the will of the majority as morally required, because the nation is primary. War, then, is the expression of an egotistical violence performed in the name of a group that has made itself God: primary and immune while simultaneously victim of threats and danger. In fact, one way to view the formation and justification of nation-states is as the repositories of violence: the state holds the authority to engage in overt, physical violence in order to deal with domestic and international threats through its exercise of the police function and its ability to wage wars. Whatever else states may do, their existence is justified fundamentally through their role in protecting the security—especially the physical and material security—of their citizens.

In order for a state to rule, then, contemporary political theory holds that there must be a base level of consensus on the part of individuals to be ruled, that is, to accept the laws of the state as both legitimate and binding. In order for this consensus to be reached, there must be a significant level of political homogeneity, ways in which separate individuals come to see themselves as part of the same whole. Some level of identity must be established between the people and the state in order for the state to be "theirs." Pledging allegiance, voting, and other civic signs and duties are important precisely because they are practices that assert and reaffirm this common identity.

What I have been trying to do in this all-too-brief discussion is argue that Bonhoeffer and Orwell are right, though incomplete, in their criticism of pacifism. The situation is far worse than they indicate.

—∾—

The Anecdote That Would Have Been Prologue If It Had Been Placed at the Beginning

Many years ago when I was much younger and more foolish and had more time on my hands than I knew what to do with, I would spend most of my time hanging out with my few friends in one of their basements. Even though it was the seventies, which we all recall with either fond nostalgia or horrified disbelief as a decade of sex, drugs, and rock 'n' roll, for my friends and me it was only a time of the music. None of the few girls we knew would even consider dating any of us, and we were either too naive or timid to experiment with any drugs other than beer, wine, and cigarettes. So we spent many hours in basements pretending to be cool, nursing cans of Rheingold or Ballantine beer and listening to rock.

Of course there was also television, but we didn't watch it all that often, only on those rare occasions when at least three of the four of us found the music boring or were restless. One Saturday night in particular stands out as one of those occasions. We turned off the stereo and began to flip the dial to see if anything was on that was interesting, and since it was around 11:00 p.m., our choices were very limited, because we certainly were too cool to watch the late news. We stopped when we found a music show on the Public Broadcasting station.

Austin City Limits is now a venerable fixture on PBS, but back around thirty years ago it was something startling to the four of us. In our snug New York City suburb and with our steady diet of the Stones, the Doors, and Hendrix, we had no idea that country-and-western music could be about anything other than trains and nasal lamentations on broken hearts; nor did we know that the music itself could be, well, so listenable.

I don't recall now who first had the idea of hitting the road to attend one of the shows. I don't think any of us at the time had even heard of Ferlinghetti, let alone read him. Whichever one of us it was, it did not take too long for us to reach a consensus that we should pool whatever money we could get together and go to Austin, Texas. We spent a few hours arguing about the route, though. We had all seen Easy Rider a good number of times, and we were convinced that the citizens as well as the police in Georgia, Alabama, and Mississippi would just love to get their hands on four shaggy-headed punks from New York. Delusions of Dennis Hopper. So we decided that instead of a southern route we ought to drive due west to Nebraska and then turn left.

For reasons I do not now comprehend, it never occurred to any of us to actually get a map. I think Peter was the most farsighted of all, because I seem to recall his asking just where in Texas Austin was located. I think we mocked his caution as a way to mask our embarrassment at not knowing the answer. Finally, either Jimmy or the Fish (so named because he resembled a halibut when he smiled) came upon the fine idea of just driving to Dallas and asking directions once we got there.

Then came the day. One morning before rush hour began, and loaded with a case of Pepsi and a carton of cigarettes, we all piled into Jimmy's Plymouth, popped in a tape of Jethro Tull's *Aqualung*, and headed hell-bent for the George Washington Bridge and points west.

We broke down in Harrisburg, Pennsylvania, and rode a Greyhound bus back home.

———〜〜〜———

The key element in both Bonhoeffer's and Orwell's discussions that I discussed earlier centers upon the notion of success—Bonhoeffer arguing that success needs to be pursued out of necessity, and Orwell that Hitler's Germany cannot be successfully overcome through pacifism. In both of their cases—and I think for many of us—one of the major difficulties with pacifism is that it is ineffectual. Pacifism is ineffectual according to this view both in a moral sense, because it regards success as ethically neutral, as well as in a pragmatic sense, in that nonviolence in the face of evil is the same as surrendering to evil. Bonhoeffer and Orwell are each making connections between actions that are effective and an outcome that is successful, as though one leads inevitably to the other. I am not sure the connection is that clear in all cases. Nor is it obvious to me that it is impossible for success to arise out of ineffective actions. Nonetheless, the issues Bonhoeffer and Orwell raise must lead us to consider what it means for actions to be effective and therefore successful, or ineffective and therefore failures.

It is obvious that some actions can be called "instrumental" in that they are important or necessary to reach one's goal or purpose. Sometimes we act the way we do not because of anything about the action itself but because we want to achieve something else outside the action. This can be a useful way of clarifying some actions, because it provides us with a relatively easy way to evaluate them. If we wish to evaluate actions of this type, a particular methodology suggests itself, the steps of which could be performed in any order. We have to determine what the person doing the action (usually called the "agent") wanted to achieve by doing it; then, whether or not she achieved it. Next, we need to consider how well she achieved it—that is, efficiently, in a timely manner, etc. Finally, and not least of all, we need to determine whether the achievement of her purpose was worth the effort in the first place.

The result of considering the action in this manner serves as a way to confer value on both the action and the agent herself. Insofar as we consider any person as an agent, the actions she performs and our evaluation of them is a key way to both understand and evaluate the agent herself. There is a transitivity in instrumental actions that affects how we regard the persons who perform them. In many ways both Bonhoeffer and Orwell rely on this transitivity, as their judgments about pacifistic actions transform into judgments about pacifists. Nor is this transitivity necessarily something bad or something we should avoid, as long as we recognize that evaluating the effectiveness of actions is simply a method to evaluate a single aspect of what it is to be a person.

By using this standard method of evaluation, my friends' and my intention to drive that old, poorly maintained Plymouth to Dallas in order to attend a show in Austin was, even with the moderating influence of the intervening decades, so ridiculously ineffective as to be laughable. There was no aspect of that complex action that we undertook that was in any way successful, except perhaps for the playing of the Tull tape.

This way of regarding actions as instrumental and using the goal as the yardstick to evaluate them is appropriate and useful if we are considering such goals as building houses, making pancakes, or taking car trips to the Southwest. But there are other times and situations when the results of actions have little or no bearing on the proper evaluation of acts or persons. Not all actions are instrumental actions, and not all instrumental actions are instrumental in the same way. Simply put, there are some actions that may be worth doing solely in terms of themselves without any reference to their effects and results. And, as a corollary, there are some actions that are not worth doing—that should not be performed at all—even if the effects and results of those actions may be desired and willed by most persons. One example comes to mind that is especially germane to the discussion in this book.

It is difficult to evaluate Jesus's ministry as successful in almost any respect. It is hard to consider most things about Jesus's life and work simply: there are nearly two millennia's worth of commentary and analysis that one ought to consult if one desires to be comprehensive. Nonetheless, if we are indeed called to follow him and to act the way he showed us, we do have to ask what kinds of actions he performed. How are we to understand the types of actions he engaged in, and why he did the things scripture tells us, as well as why he did not act in ways we might expect?

That said, at least one aspect of Jesus's ministry in particular has long been puzzling to me. When I was a child and did not yet know what kinds of questions I should not ask, I asked my parish priest why Jesus did not decide to perform *more* miracles and cure everybody of everything that ailed them. I had just started paying attention to the Gospel readings during Mass, and I was impressed that he could cure the blind and the paralyzed; I could even envision the paralyzed man picking up his mat and walking away. I don't think I understood what *hemorrhaging* means at that time, so I didn't really appreciate his stopping the woman's bleeding, but I did get the point when he brought Lazarus back to life. What I did not understand then and still grapple with now whenever I allow myself to wonder about it, is that Jesus evidently decided not to eliminate all pain, all suffering, and all death in Israel. Clearly he had the power, and he also had the opportunity, as he walked through the countryside and visited all of those towns, villages, and cities. So why did he only occasionally have the will?

I don't recall in detail the answer the priest gave me, but I can clearly remember the look on his face after I asked that question: it was a look that encouraged me not to pursue whatever his answer was going to be with another question. What I do remember, vague as it is, is that the main point of his response was that Jesus's ministry was *not* about cures, healings, and raising the dead, despite the emphasis the Evangelists appeared to place on those acts in the Gospels. What this response leads me to is the next, inevitable set of questions I did not ask the priest: if not the elimination of suffering, then what was the point of his ministry? Why did Jesus come in the way he did, and just what did he hope to accomplish?

The most immediate answer that comes to mind is the easiest, but it does raise further difficulties. Jesus came to proclaim the good news of our salvation and to exemplify the love and mercy of the Father. (As I write this, it occurs to me that understanding what this answer means is not easy at all.) But it is not clear to me why he couldn't effect a few more cures and healings along the way, especially since he taught us that we should alleviate suffering and take care of the poorest among us. There needs to be some kind of explanation for reconciling his ministry with his failure to do quite a bit more to ease the material problems of his people.

I have put this question to a few friends and colleagues who are much more learned than I am in theology and scripture, and invariably the first response I get is that I am wrong. Jesus certainly did help all of those in pain who came to him and asked that he use his power to heal them. Lazarus, of course, was an exception to this apparent rule, since he had already died, yet even so, others intervened on his behalf, much as the Roman centurion asked Jesus on behalf of his daughter. Jesus always responded favorably to all of them.

All of this is, of course, true, but it strikes me as a bit beside the point. Jesus frequently exhorted his disciples and the people of Israel to greater faith, and he rewarded the faithful for their demonstrations of belief. Healing those who believe in his message certainly does make sense, since he assures us that whatever one who has faith asks for will be granted.

But at the same time, this seems to be a problematic criterion. If Jesus is our exemplar and we ought to imitate him, and if the only way one could have received the material assistance of Jesus was by a prior declaration of faith, then these two statements would seem to imply that the ones Christians should endeavor to help out of their material suffering would be only those who had already come to believe in Jesus as Savior. Yet that restriction on Christian benevolence does not appear anywhere in the Gospels or Epistles, and it further runs counter to the practices of the church over the millennia. I am unaware of the church imposing any such restrictions on the aid we provide that has not been subsequently condemned, much as we have never refused to preach the good news to those who have not professed belief. The Christian church has counted as saints those who, in the name of the Lord, have gone out and fed the hungry, clothed the naked, and served the sick and dying no matter what faith, if any, those in need expressed. It is very difficult for me to believe that a St. Francis or a St. Clare or a Mother Teresa is somehow more in tune with what the gospel means than was Jesus himself. So to say that faith was in some way a requirement for Jesus to act benevolently—and that is the clear implication of pointing out that Jesus was asked to use his power—seems way too problematic to provide a sufficient answer to the question.

As I have indicated, another difficulty in understanding why Jesus did not act more benevolently is that effecting cures for loathsome and intractable diseases like leprosy would seem to be an incredibly effective marketing technique. Not that long ago, Philip Morris would have small packages of cigarettes distributed on street corners so that prospective customers would be encouraged to change brands. In addition, to use a slightly different resurrection story, word of the success of Viagra and Cialis has led to more sales and larger profits for the respective pharmaceutical companies. It would seem, then, that if Jesus wished to get more people to believe in his message of love, mercy, salvation, and the arrival of the kingdom, he would give them significant and tangible reasons to pay more serious attention to him and his message. He would have attracted a greater audience, sold the message more easily, and made his claims to be Messiah easier to swallow. I imagine that if Palestine had conducted proper polling at the time, Jesus's name recognition and approval ratings would have been very high after feeding the five thousand. These practical considerations seem so obvious that they just make his failure to act in those ways even more puzzling, especially considering the condition of the Israelites as a subject people who suffered significantly at the hands of the Romans as well as from microbes.

Nonetheless, Jesus did not act that way. He cured relatively few people that we know about, and he seemed to be somewhat indifferent to the rest. Pain, suffering, and disease still ravaged the Israelites when he walked among them, even the children he favored. And I would also guess that the cures he did perform were probably not as efficacious as they could have been. For example, we must assume that at some point in time Lazarus died once and for all. Even though Jesus brought Lazarus back to life, the Lord did not decide to make him either immortal or impervious to subsequent ailments.

No matter what ultimately happened to Lazarus, it seems clear that Jesus would have been more successful in preaching salvation than he was if only he had decided to act more benevolently. It is difficult for me to believe that he would not have demonstrated to all the people of Israel that he was the Messiah, eventually converting the entirety of the empire by simply eliminating disease, disability, and death wherever it existed.

All of these issues bring us to the next and most overarching questions of all: just how effective was Jesus, anyway? How do we and how should we evaluate the effectiveness of his ministry? Can we even consider the life of

Jesus a success? These may seem to be a very strange series of questions when we consider how rapidly Christianity spread throughout the empire and beyond. Arguably, the spread of Christianity is even more impressive than the spread of its two closest rivals through the centuries, that is, Islam and market capitalism. And insofar as Islam recognizes Jesus as a great prophet, one could well argue that Jesus's ministry was an astonishing success.

I am not so sure.

One of the first things we ought to do in examining these questions is determine what counts as Jesus's ministry. If we are going to evaluate actions in terms of their effects, we need to be very clear about what counts as a relevant action, what counts as an effect, and which effects are connected to which actions. After all, it is certainly plausible to attribute the spread of the church in that first hundred years more to the activities of Paul and Silas than to Jesus himself.

As with so much else, an objection most likely arises at this point. Even if one has only a cursory knowledge of scripture, one knows that a primary argument of the Letter to the Hebrews indicates that Jesus's ministry is not at an end even now, that it persists through time and that he continues to be the mediator of the new covenant (see 9:15, for example). Nonetheless, we Christians take Jesus's earthly life as normative—giving us the most significant example of how to live our lives—so I will take the examination of the question in that spirit. If Jesus's life and ministry as described by the evangelists is supposed to be normative, it should also be open to the same kind of evaluation that Bonhoeffer and Orwell engage in during their critical examinations.

With this in mind, it seems to me that what counts as Jesus's ministry for our purposes has one of two answers. His ministry encompassed his life from his baptism to either his crucifixion or his ascension into heaven.

The second question centers on what Jesus hoped to accomplish through his ministry. Clearly, as I implied with my troublesome question to the parish priest, his goal was not to alleviate the material suffering of the people of God. His activities on that score were too sporadic and appear to be ancillary to his primary intention. Jesus came to preach the arrival of the kingdom and also to bring God's people a message of repentance, return, and hope. So, given what he did as recounted in the Gospels, and considering the effects of his actions, can we say that Jesus was successful?

I tend to doubt it.

If Jesus's ministry ended with his crucifixion, then it was an abysmal failure. The situation at the time of his death was exceedingly bleak: all of his disciples had abandoned him, except for John; the disciple in charge of finances, Judas Iscariot, betrayed him to the authorities; and his chief disciple, Peter, not only abandoned him but even denied ever having known him. Further, the people of God to whom he preached, and some of whom he fed, preferred to save the criminal Barabbas rather than him. In the days immediately following his execution, ten of his eleven disciples, handpicked and presumably trained over a number of years, were cowering in a locked room fearing arrest, imprisonment, and death. We have no idea what the missing apostle Thomas was doing during his break from cowering, but it's a safe bet he was not out proclaiming the Word during his excursion. Our first alternative results in the conclusion that Jesus's ministry ended up a failure, with no one exhibiting even a hint of the faith he taught, preached, and exemplified.

The other alternative is scarcely more laudatory. If we include the forty days after his resurrection as part of his ministry, then Jesus is a bit more successful, but not by much. He spent those days rebuilding or reinforcing the faith of the disciples (though we must note that the number of apostles had been diminished by 8.3 percent with the suicide of Judas). Even that he had to do by actually appearing to them, which earned them a rebuke for their obstinate unbelief (Mark 16:14). Thus either Jesus's ministry was an abysmal failure, with all left in ruins, or he succeeded in reconvincing eleven persons of the truth they had accepted previously but then rejected, which probably counts as an abject failure.

Now certainly some are going to protest that I have missed the point, particularly the point I had made previously: the goal of Jesus's ministry was to preach the arrival of the kingdom and to bring God's people the message of repentance, return, and hope. At least regarding that goal he was successful.

I don't think so. The mere annunciation of these messages could hardly be significant enough. By this standard, if Jesus had stood on a rock by the Sea of Galilee and proclaimed his message to the water and stones and no one had heard him, he would have been "successful." The point of his goal of preaching the Word is rather that the hearts and souls of humans would be transformed, and that transformation either did not occur or occurred for so few that the result amounts to the same thing: he failed.

I am doing nothing more in these paragraphs than applying the same criterion to Jesus's ministry that I applied to the abortive road trip of thirty years ago. Either that road trip was an abysmal failure in that we did not arrive at the place we planned to, or it was an abject failure because, while we did not achieve our goal, we at least arrived back home safely and with a few dollars left over. Jesus failed in much the same way we failed, and I am hard put to come up with a way to describe Jesus's ministry that saves it from disaster. I suppose one could argue that the subsequent success of the disciples should be attributed to Jesus, since Jesus was the original source of the message, yet that does not seem to work either. If my sons are able, at some future date after I have died, to attend a performance of *Austin City Limits,* I don't think it at all accurate to say that I will have finally succeeded in my goal, even if they got the idea to attend the show from my story. Rather, it seems the success would be theirs, or even that they will have succeeded in achieving the same aim that I had failed to achieve. There is simply no way for me to consider Jesus's ministry a success.

To make matters worse—though I admit that seems a difficult thing to do—Jesus was also a peacemaker, which leaves him open to the threefold problem of pacifism as expressed by Bonhoeffer and Orwell. To recapitulate that problem, Bonhoeffer and Orwell claim that

1. By refusing to engage in violence, the pacifist ultimately helps the cause of evil.
2. Pacifism is hypocritical because pacifists enjoy the fruit of violence in the defense of their security.
3. Pacifism as a strategy to combat evil is ineffectual and doomed to be unsuccessful.

Since I believe what I have said above about the ineffectiveness of Jesus's ministry is unambiguously applicable to the more particular claim made in (3), I will not devote any more time to that issue. Rather, I will focus my remarks on the first two aspects of the problem of pacifism and briefly examine how Jesus fares in light of that critique.

To what extent should we consider Jesus a hypocrite according to the second claim? It certainly appears to be the case that through most of his earthly ministry Jesus enjoyed the safety and protection of the Roman Empire. And we must also bear in mind that the security that enabled Jesus to travel throughout Palestine and preach peace and forgiveness was purchased through the violence and the threat of violence the empire held against all it considered malefactors. Similarly, Jesus enjoyed the stability and structure first-century Judaism provided as well. Insofar as Jesus worked to undermine and subvert those civil and religious authorities under whom he derived those significant benefits, Jesus appears to be a hypocrite of the first order.

If we consider that the civil and religious authorities of first-century Palestine were, to some large extent, forces of evil—the Roman authorities in their political and military domination and oppression of Israel, and the Pharisees in their attempts to undermine Jesus's teachings and evangelization, as well as in their conspiracy to judicially murder him—then it would follow that Jesus's refusal to engage in violence against those powers ultimately aided them in their persecution of the early church and in their other evil endeavors. In fact, the only time when Jesus seems even remotely to use violence is recounted in the story of his confrontation in the temple (Matt. 21:12f; Mark 11:15f; Luke 19:45f). Each of the Evangelists' accounts maintains that Jesus drove out all of those who were selling and buying in the temple, but none of them reports that he used violence to accomplish this. Driving someone out of a place could easily be achieved through moral suasion in some circumstances. Matthew and Mark go on to offer the description that Jesus then "upset the tables of the money changers and the seats of the dove sellers." John's account of this episode (2:13–17), on the other hand, includes a description of Jesus "making a whip out of a cord and driving them out of the temple." Yet it seems largely symbolic—lumping the merchants with the sheep and cattle, all to be shooed away from the holy place. While these actions can be counted as violent ones, I do not think they rise to the level of violent resistance to evil as advocated by Bonhoeffer and Orwell.

Jesus's nonviolence and pacifistic reaction to evil is much less ambiguous when he is arrested in Gethsemane. Accepting without argument that the arrest, trial, and execution of Jesus were barbarously evil acts, it is significant that Jesus reproved his follower (identified as Peter in John 18:10) for drawing his sword and cutting off the ear of the high priest's servant:

> Jesus then said, "Put your sword back, for all who draw the sword will die by the sword. Or do you think that I cannot appeal to my Father, who would promptly send more than twelve legions of angels to my defence? But then, how would the scriptures be fulfilled that say this is the way it must be?" (Matt. 26:52–54)

In John 18:11, Jesus puts it slightly differently: "Put your sword back in its scabbard; am I not to drink the cup that the Father has given me?" Significantly, in Luke's account (Luke 22:51) Jesus then heals the ear of the servant, rising above the violence of his arrest, as well as the violent resistance Peter displayed against the evil, with peace and healing. The result of Jesus's peacemaking in this instance is his execution and the flight of his disciples.

If we are to evaluate this episode with reference to the criteria that both Bonhoeffer and Orwell accept, then Jesus's nonviolent response, as well as his active prevention of Peter's resistance to evil, is tantamount to tacit approval and support of the evil action. If we were to use that standard, then Jesus is no longer victim but accomplice; he is not simply accepting his role as sacrificial offering but rather is an accessory to evil and to those actions whose effects were so devastating in their immediate practical consequences.

The obvious answer to all of these absurd conclusions is not that there is something fundamentally misguided about applying the standard of evaluation to only the immediate results of his ministry. Bonhoeffer and Orwell are both utilizing a standard of evaluating pacifistic responses to evil that focuses on the relatively immediate practical effects of those actions. If that is the standard we are to use, then the life of Jesus fails the test.

I hope what I have been trying to do in the body of this chapter has been clear. My point in trying to evaluate the life of the Lord has not been an attempt to show that faithfulness is some defective or unattainable ideal that no one, not even Jesus, can live up to. Rather, I am trying to show that it is precisely that standard of evaluation that we commonly use that is defective and ought not be applied either to Jesus's ministry or to our discipleship. In his ministry, Jesus overturns and replaces the standard of evaluation that the secular world gives us with another, different standard. Jesus had the capability to resist the arresting mob by calling on the legions of angels—and he identifies them clearly as "legions" because that is the primary military unit of the Roman Empire. This he refuses to do. Instead, he repays violence and evil with love.

Through his life and ministry, Jesus teaches us to live our lives as he did his. We are called to a life of faithfulness to the Word, with forgiveness, peace, and love toward all, especially to our enemies and evildoers. The standard by which we will be judged and by which we should evaluate ourselves is not the pragmatic standard of the world. Being church and being disciples of Christ is not like driving a Plymouth to Dallas. While the world should look upon Jesus's life and ministry as failures and what he calls us to be as foolish, futile, and contrary to our nature, the Word teaches the church a new meaning of *success* and calls us to follow him.

Seventh Meditation

Luke 12:22–32

Then he said to his disciples, "That is why I am telling you not to worry about your life and what you are to eat, nor about your body and how you are to clothe it. For life is more than food, and the body more than clothing. Think of the ravens. They do not sow or reap; they have no storehouses and no barns; yet God feeds them. And how much more are you worth than the birds! Can any of you, however much you worry, add a single cubit to your span of life? If a very small thing is beyond your powers, why worry about the rest? Think how the flowers grow; they never have to spin or weave; yet, I assure you, not even Solomon in all his royal robes was clothed like one of them. Now if that is how God clothes a flower which is growing wild today and is thrown into the furnace tomorrow, how much more will he look after you, who have so little faith! But you must not set your hearts on things to eat and things to drink; nor must you worry. It is the gentiles of this world who set their hearts on all these things. Your Father well knows you need them. No; set your hearts on his kingdom, and these other things will be given to you as well.

"There is no need to be afraid, little flock, for it has pleased your Father to give you the kingdom."

■ Lord, help me to remember that I am always in your presence.

So many of your children have written on this passage and the parallel one at Matthew 6:25, especially my favorites Kierkegaard and von Balthasar, but I still find myself anxious in spite of your words. And because of them.

147

I am not worried about clothing—anyone who looks at me can tell you that—or about food, maybe because I have so much that I have come to take these and the other necessaries for granted. I think I worry about what is scarce, not abundant, and what lies outside my power to get. The passage before this tells about the rich man who built larger barns to store his grain and thus becomes even wealthier. You took him that night, and all the treasures he cared for and saved did him no good at all.

So part of what you are telling me is that I should pay more attention to my relationship with you and following in your path than I do to the material possessions I have. And I see the truth in that; I spend much more time concerned about objects—those I have and those I want—my job and deadlines, that my focus and concern sometimes seem to be everywhere but on the most important, the defining, feature of my life.

I take that rebuke and warning, but that is not the part of this passage that causes me worry and anxiety.

I think in some ways that you want to comfort us with your examples of the ravens and the flowers. They don't worry or fret about their future, and the Father takes care of them. And earlier in this chapter of Luke you speak about the five sparrows that can be bought for a couple of small coins, and how they are not forgotten in God's sight. Please excuse me, but if you wanted me not to be anxious, why did you choose those creatures as examples? I would worry much less if instead you pointed to the eagles and the owls, and used the image of an oak (or even a cedar of Lebanon). Let's face it, eagles and owls are at the top of the food chain; there are no threats to them, and they manage to find food to eat and, I presume, die happy deaths of old age. And, as symbol, the eagle represents strength and ferocity so well that my country uses it as a symbol for itself, much as the legions of Rome did when you walked with us. The owl, then as now, is the symbol of wisdom and intelligence; it was the beloved bird of Minerva. Likewise an oak tree—and here I am not sure Palestine had oaks—or a cedar of Lebanon is majestic: both dominate landscapes and symbolize strength and perseverance and are beloved for generations because their lives are long.

But instead of these you give us flowers, sparrows, and ravens. The flowers are pretty, yes, but they don't last. You yourself say that they are destined for the furnace. And I don't know why folks in your day would buy sparrows, even for a few pennies. The only reasons I can think of are that they were intended either for the temple sacrifices or for the dinner pot. Ravens aren't much better. They symbolize death and eat carrion: they clean our streets of roadkill and, I was told or read somewhere, they are pets at the Tower of London because they remind us of the executions that were held there. What this amounts to, Lord, is you telling me not to worry by focusing on weeds, chicken fingers, and the birds of death.

I should be at ease, then, because the Father's mindfulness of these creatures? He may well be mindful of them, but they don't have especially wonderful futures, destined, as they are, for the furnace, the knife, and meals of rotting corpses. Just how is the Father taking care of them, and in what way am I to be consoled by this darkling and depressing picture? It's as though you are telling me that I should not worry about a heart attack: "Be at ease because you will be dead from cancer long before that."

I know I will die, and I know that I can't know when. It seems that I have been anxious about it only periodically and only seriously since I turned forty-five. Frankly, I try not to think about it much, and when I do I prefer to think about an eagle's death or an oak tree's—something rather gradual: a slow, steady decline after an especially long and dominating life. Better I should think about the foolish rich guy building new barns than about ravens and flowering weeds.

And the Father is mindful of me, is looking after me even as I am being readied for the furnace. What is that supposed to mean? I would think it should mean he will save me from the furnace, but then he wouldn't even save you from a horrible death when you were much younger than I am now. That makes me anxious. I am to be like you, to take up my cross and follow you, and define success as you did. If I may be frank, that is not such a delightful prospect.

So, let's bottom-line this thing, because I am getting more and more anxious the more I go on, and there's a crow sitting outside my window right now. (Nice touch, Jesus.) And I am weak and weary, to boot. We both know where I am headed and what some tomorrow will bring; the only thing lacking is the details. You promise me eternal life if I am faithful; and if I am faithful I can also expect to be insulted, reviled, outcast, and killed. The message I am getting from this passage is that sparrows, ravens, and flowers are being just what they should be, and that even though their futures hold death, they are not focused on that. They are not even conscious of their deaths, or perhaps they expect it in the same way we expect the coming of tomorrow: so much a matter of course that it warrants no attention. By being what they are meant to be, they are beloved by the Father. If I am what I am meant to be, then the Father will look after me as well, more beloved and precious. My focus in this life should be only on that.

I am mouthing the words I think I should say; that whole paragraph comes from my head and my spiritual reading rather than my soul. Perhaps they are Stanley Hauerwas's words, since I plagiarize him so much. I cannot avoid anxiety about tomorrow; I just do not have enough faith that I can endure what I cannot control. And I have to wonder how much of my "faith" is a mouthing of the words I think I should believe. I want to set my heart on the kingdom, but the kingdom of heaven seems so far away, while clothes, food, comfort, and the esteem of my brothers and sisters are so close. The Father is mindful of me and shall take care of me, but I want it to be about the things I am mindful of and care about. You and I diverge so much on what we consider important and worth doing that I alternate between wondering when I will ever learn and wondering when you will ever learn. All you want is for me to be faithful today; and I want to be faithful today; and today I also worry about what that will amount to tomorrow. Help my unbelief.

Bless my mind to illuminate me with your wisdom;
Bless my lips to allow me to speak your word;
And bless my heart that I might live the gospel.

7

The Christian Response

■ At this juncture it is time for me to respond to the Hitler question: how should Christians respond to the kind of evil Hitler represents if just war theory and supreme emergencies are precluded, and if we live with a different meaning of success?

We must live faithfully; we must be humble in our faith and truthful in what we say and do; we must repay evil with good; and we must be peacemakers. This may also mean as a result that the evildoers will kill us. Then, we shall also die.

That's it. There is nothing else—or rather, anything else is only a footnote to this. We are called to live the kingdom as he proclaimed it and be his disciples, come what may. We are, in his words, flowers flourishing and growing wild today, and tomorrow destined for the furnace. We are God's people, living by faith.

The gospel is clear and simple, and I know what the response to the Hitler question must be. And I desperately want to avoid this conclusion. When my time comes, I may well trot out every nuanced argument I can develop, or seek for a way out in St. Thomas Aquinas or Paul Ramsey. This would serve me and my fear, my hypocrisy, and my faithlessness very well. But I would not be telling the truth or living as I ought and as I am called to live.

Eighth Meditation

Romans 7:15–25

I do not understand my own behaviour; I do not act as I mean to, but I do things that I hate. While I am acting as I do not want to, I still acknowledge the law as good, so it is not myself acting, but the sin which lives in me. And really, I know of nothing good living in me—in my natural self, that is—for though the will to do what is good is in me, the power to do it is not: the good thing I want to do, I never do; the evil thing which I do not want—that is what I do. But every time I do what I do not want to, then it is not myself acting, but the sin that lives in me.

So I find this rule: that for me, where I want to do nothing but good, evil is close at my side. In my inmost self I dearly love God's law, but I see that acting on my body there is a different law which battles against the law in my mind. So I am brought to be a prisoner of that law of sin which lives inside my body.

What a wretched man I am! Who will rescue me from this body doomed to death? God—thanks be to him—through Jesus Christ our Lord.

So it is that I myself with my mind obey the law of God, but in my disordered nature I obey the law of sin.

■ Lord, help me to remember that I am always in your presence.

When I read this passage, Lord, I am both relieved and pained. I am relieved that what I so often feel when I examine my life is something that St. Paul also felt: the great disconnect between how I want to live—as your disciple—and how I actually live, which is quite a bit less than what we both expect of me. And I am in pain at the same time, because this remains true and it is quite frustrating, like my frequent attempts to stop smoking and swearing. I function under two laws, and while it is true that my attempts to live the gospel often end in failure, neither can I sin freely, because while I am sinning I know that I am called to a better life. It is the worst of both worlds: a failure as both saint and sinner.

What is it that pulls me away and in another direction than the one you call me to? Paul says it is my natural self that lacks the power. And he also says that when I do what I do not want that it is not myself but the sin that lives in me. I want to jump on that sentence as a way to bypass my own guilt and responsibility, because it seems to leave my self immune, even though I am not sure what it is that's inside me that counts as my self. Is my self that part of me that *wants* to do your will, and if so, then why does it lack the power? It occurs to me that perhaps the self lacks only the power to do good but retains the power to do evil. Yet Paul says that it is not the self but the sin, and I can't help but wonder what the sin is in relation to my self. It seems that Paul is not saying that my self is evil—probably because it is the self that wills me to do good. But the sin that somehow cohabits my being has the power to attract me, perhaps, so that I obey its law rather than the law I recognize as yours. Paul says that the self is a prisoner to this sin living within, that the disordered self cannot win the struggle between what I want and what I do. (Do you have any idea how hard it is to keep all of this straight?)

As I reflect, though, I do think that sometimes I will to follow your law and that sometimes I also do it. I do not feel this conflict all the time—only on occasion do I see how my self is touched by disorder, confusion, and the kind of anguish Paul speaks of. So is it that the sin that resides within me only occasionally has the power to drive a wedge, not only between us but also between these separate aspects of my own person?

I paused for a while to think about that last paragraph and the battle that takes place within me that I am aware of only on occasion. Perhaps the battle persists even when I am not aware of it. And what I think of as the law of sin surrendering to your law really works the other way around. Paul says that the "good thing I want to do, I never do," so maybe when I do not feel the struggle, conflict, and confusion, it is really the case that I have subordinated your call to the sin that lives within me.

There is a peace that comes, Paul says later on, to those who live in the Spirit, yet there is also a peace in the death that comes from our natural inclinations. Those cannot be the same thing, but I do not know how to distinguish the peace of death from the peace of the Spirit and eternal life. I know that one is nothing, and the other everything, but how do I see which is which here and now? I want the Spirit of God to make a home in me, and I want to be guided by the Spirit, but I don't know how.

Paul tells me that you have rescued me, but truly I feel more lost, more of a hostage to my natural self and inclinations than I feel redeemed and at peace. I have always distrusted those who sing "Glory! Glory!" and those who tell me what a friend they have found in you. I neither feel nor see nor understand what your friendship is or how it works to save me. All well and good for Paul to say that we have no obligation to human nature to be dominated by it (8:12), but I don't know how not to be dominated by my nature. Isn't that what nature is supposed to do—dominate and direct? And I do not know how to let you in so that you direct me. I pray to give you my mind and my will and my memory, but still it seems that the sin within me is what directs what I do.

I swear you frustrate me. I have the words and I don't understand them; I see the puzzle and have no clue how the solution works. I hear that I am a child of God, but I feel orphaned; I hear I am destined for glory, but I see all of what I do as sinful and look forward to nothing but death. I am waiting for you to come back as you came to the upper room on Easter, because I do not have enough faith to trust you. I don't even have enough faith to trust myself, even to knowing what I am doing when I am doing it. Paul says that in hope we already have salvation (8:24), so is the hope enough? Is my desire that you save me enough? My inmost self wanting to live by your Word and obey the law of God: is that enough for the Spirit to make a house in me?

I wish you would give me a sign. I know. You already have. But it isn't enough.

Bless my mind to illuminate me with your wisdom.
Bless my lips to allow me to speak your word.
And bless my heart that I might live the gospel.

8

Elaboration

Prologue

For a brief time I worked as a Cancer Care Technician in a small hospital that treated only terminal cancer patients. Although the job title was a lofty one and implies impressive training and skills, those of us who were hired as C.C. Techs were essentially nurse's aides. Our duties mainly involved taking our patients' vital signs—temperature, blood pressure, respiration—making beds with those tight hospital corners (I never mastered that) and, of course, cleaning bedpans. Every now and then it was necessary for us to massage patients' backs to try to prevent bedsores for the nonambulatory, give sponge baths and shaves, and even change the dressings on their wounds.

I met Mr. Levinsky early on in my time there, principally because I had to learn the intricacies of changing his dressings. Actually, as I reflect on it, I think the head nurse of my ward, tired of the frequent turnover of male C.C. Techs, wanted to determine as soon as possible if I could stomach this duty. I don't recall the kind of cancer that was killing Mr. Levinsky, but both of his legs had been amputated above the knees. His stumps were red and raw like a bottom round roast, and they oozed. His dressings had to be applied carefully so that the tape would not irritate the skin on his thighs more than was necessary.

But Mr. Levinsky was challenging as a patient not only because of his stumps—amputations took some getting used to but were more or less normal on this ward. Mr. Levinsky was also "confused." Sometimes in the latter stages of dying, when the patient's cancer metastasizes to the brain, the patient will become disoriented and even incoherent. This was affecting Mr. Levinsky to such an extent that he did not know where he was or why, nor did he understand what was happening to him even during the simplest procedures, like sponge baths. Often when a C.C. Tech would take Mr. Levinsky's blood pressure, he would yell his protests and cusswords at the top of his lungs; he would thrash about and try to remove the BP cuff. Even though his yelling and movements were fairly weak, they were invariably disconcerting and upsetting, especially to a new C.C. Tech. In showing me how to change his dressings, however, the head nurse moved quickly and efficiently and did not appear to be disturbed or even the least bit distracted by Mr. Levinsky's actions. She was done and packed up in a few minutes. Later in the day, just before my shift ended, I changed Mr. Levinsky's dressings under the supervision of the head nurse. Mr. Levinsky was quiet and cooperative; I was awkward and slow, using much more tape than was necessary, but I finally managed to do an acceptable job.

Not surprisingly, the next morning Mr. Levinsky was assigned to me, and I had to change his dressings as part of my normal routine. And do it alone. We were all overworked, and the head nurse had other duties to attend to. I rolled my cart into Mr. Levinsky's room and was speaking cheerfully and soothingly to him in that maple-syrupy voice nurse's aides assume, trying to head off his outburst of confused complaint and thrashing protest. My eyes were fixed upon his stumps, and my mind was rehearsing the process as I approached his bed. Almost immediately as I reached his bedside, though, I noticed a particularly acrid smell. Mr. Levinsky had diarrhea and had fouled his bed. He was lying in a large pool of feces. Obviously, before I could change the dressings, I had to clean Mr. Levinsky and change his bed sheets.

I went to fetch clean bed linen, a pan of warm water, and some soap. Even though I was new on the job, I had changed the fouled sheets of bed-restricted patients before, so I proceeded to do so in the manner

I had learned. I rolled Mr. Levinsky onto his left side so that he was against the bed rail. The feces extended from the base of his neck to the top of his thighs; he was covered in it. Because he was unsteady against the rail, I held him up with my left hand as I washed and cleaned his back with my right hand. After applying some disinfectant to his back, I turned to get the clean sheets and Mr. Levinsky rolled back into the pool of feces on his bed. At this point, Mr. Levinsky began to yell. He was also covered again with the foul, sticky feces. I decided I should have changed his sheets first, so I rolled Mr. Levinsky on his side again, held him there, removed the soiled bottom sheet and replaced it with a clean one. I turned to get the soap, water, sponge, and disinfectant to wash Mr. Levinsky's back. He then rolled onto his back, soiling the sheets I had just changed. Now Mr. Levinsky started to thrash. He was covered with feces. The bed was covered with feces. I was covered with feces.

We went through this process one more time. Mr. Levinsky was getting more disturbed as I proceeded with my awkwardness. I was becoming even more clumsy, unsure of myself, and inept; I was also getting dirtier. The more he would yell and thrash and call me the vilest names I have ever heard, the more upset and chest-tightened I became. Very soon I found myself confronting a strange transition of feelings: my emotions had quickly moved from a detached sympathy for him to a mounting frustration and an intense anger at him. I wanted to hit him to get him to shut up and stay where he was put. I finally had to give up, which was born more of disgust than resignation, and I rang for the nurse. I was now also embarrassed, and my pride was wounded by having to ask for help; my jaw became more clenched.

Of course, the head nurse answered the buzzer. She looked at me first, then at Mr. Levinsky, then at the pile of fecal sheets. She began, but then decided to say nothing and only shook her head. She opened the drawer of Mr. Levinsky's nightstand and took out a length of rope. She looped the rope around the top of Mr. Levinsky's right arm, rolled him onto his left side, and tied the rope to the bed rail, holding Mr. Levinsky—still yelling obscenities—in place. She cleaned his back and changed the bed sheets in a couple of minutes. Then she untied Mr. Levinsky, now calm or exhausted, gently rolled him onto his back and changed his dressings, all as I looked on helplessly. As she packed up the cart, she didn't look at me and told me to go wash up and change my clothes.

As I later walked by the nurse's station near the end of my shift, the head nurse was at the desk writing in a chart. She didn't look up but reminded me that I had to change Mr. Levinsky's dressings. All during my shift I had been trying to forget that I had wanted to pummel an old, dying, confused man, and I had to face it again. I felt the tightening of my chest and jaw as I rolled the cart into Mr. Levinsky's room; no syrup this time. I went to his bedside and took his pulse. Mr. Levinsky was dead. Mr. Levinsky wasn't the first of my patients to die and die alone, nor would he be the last, but as I stood beside his gurney as we rode the elevator to the morgue, he was the only patient I ever cried over. I don't know if I was mourning him or my shame.

———

■ Most of the people I have spoken with about that last chapter have expressed some significant dissatisfaction with it. What I can gather from their comments and reactions is that the chapter does not provide the kind of answer they wanted or expected; some have indicated that they were expecting a more "valuable" insight and, in addition, one that had a more "practical" aspect to it. The kinds of comments I received also pointed out a reaction that is so obvious that it seems hardly worth recounting: no one wants to die. If what I am saying is that following Jesus along the path of peace as his faithful disciple will probably lead to our death (which is exactly what I am saying), then there is something wrong with my understanding of the gospel. The great philosophers of our history—at least most of them—are correct: the first law of nature is self-preservation, and that means that we ought to do whatever is necessary to stay alive. It is incomprehensible that our faith might require us to pursue death.

I am not sure that states the real issue correctly, though. As Hans-Georg Gadamer has written, "For every living person there is something incomprehensible in the fact that this human consciousness capable of anticipating the future will one day come to an end" (63). There are two parts to this incomprehensibility Gadamer points to. In the first place, it seems beyond our minds to imagine our own deaths. In the second place, I don't think we can imagine a future in which we play no role, that is, we cannot foresee a time when we are nonexistent, nor a time when we will not be remembered as someone significant. The thought that we will die and, in a short time, no one will even know that we have lived, is too much for us to bear. Surely we are more important than that. But, oddly enough, behind this incomprehensibility, we are aware of it. Very few of us could name an ancestor of several generations ago, and I think for all of us there is a gap in our memory of some loved one who has died—a face, a name, the sound of a voice, what she was like when she was happy. And the memories we do have dim as time goes by.

We are frightened of this ending that shows the insignificance of our daily concerns. We are frightened of the unknown that awaits us. Even with Jesus's and the gospel's reassurance that the faithful will dwell with him throughout all eternity and that we shall always be significant in the Father's eyes, we have very many questions about what being significant in God's eyes means and even more questions about what eternity with Christ will be like. What aspects of our selves does God care about; what parts of our selves will attach to the soul that goes to heaven? Will my consciousness or my personality persist through all time, or will they change or be absorbed into some other reality; and in heaven will I have to associate with all those folks I have successfully avoided during my life on earth?

Yes, I joke about death because I fear it, and I fear it not only because I am fundamentally unsure and worried about what waits for me and for all of us after we die, but also because death itself is something that is so alien and strange that it seems unnatural. Once again, Gadamer reflects:

> The real depersonalization of death reaches deeper still in the modern hospital. Along side the loss of any public representation of what takes place, the dying and their relatives are removed from the domestic environment of the family. Death is thereby adapted to the technological business of industrial production. Looking at these changes, we can see that dying has become one of the innumerable processes of production within modern economic life, albeit a negative one. And yet there is perhaps no other experience in human life which so clearly marks the limits placed on that modern control of nature acquired through science and technology. It is precisely these enormous technological advances, with their goal of the artificial preservation of life, which reveal the absolute limit of what we can achieve. The prolongation of life finally becomes a prolongation of death and a fading away of the experience of the self. This process culminates in the gradual disappearance of the experience of death. The anaesthetic drugs developed by modern pharmaceutics can completely sedate the suffering person. The artificial maintenance of the vegetative functions of the organism makes the person into a link in the chain of causal processes. Death itself becomes like an arbitral [*sic*] reward dependent on the decision of the doctor treating the case. At the same time, all this excludes the living from attendance and participation in what is irrevocably taking place. (62)

Even though such phenomena as the hospice movement have grown in the years since Gadamer wrote this reflection in 1983, still only about 25 percent of deaths occur at home—and the number is in decline (Babiarz, 2002). The predominant tendency remains for the dying to be removed from their homes and family, and for their care to be the primary responsibility of professionals, those who are tasked with "managing" pain and easing the transition to death. I believe that Gadamer is pointing to what we generally consider to be the most disturbing element of death—even considering the fundamental uncertainties I outlined in the very beginning of this chapter. Death underlines and emphasizes our powerlessness by making it very clear how little we can do, ultimately, to control death. I think that much of our contemporary concern about "death with dignity"—and I am not sure just what that phrase is supposed to mean other than pointing to an ideal state wherein one experiences death without actually dying—is really a concern that our efforts to prolong life do in fact transform themselves into a prolongation of death with an experience of a loss of self that is evident to others. Even if we consider some of the language we use to talk about death—that it is something that "happens" to a person in a way that turning fifty, for example, does not—we can see the notion illuminated that death is something essentially outside the realm of human experience. It is something that ought to be feared in its mystery and avoided at all costs.

We think of death as something evil in itself. We do not want to die, and one of the outgrowths of these two reflections is that we fear and consider evil anything that brings us closer to death as well, like aging. We attempt to remain young through Botox injections and hair transplants, through divorce and the other myths of "starting over," in the ways we dress and comport ourselves. Aging is bad if for no other reason than that it brings us closer to death.

Nor do we want to watch others die. There may not be anything we can do to prevent death from happening, but perhaps it is sufficient if we keep it at arm's length. We can keep our distance by committing our loved ones to the professionals and also by considering the statistics. There can be distance in the numbers. I think we are much more comfortable and can remain thoughtful by looking at the total numbers of deaths from murder, drunken driving, cancer, and wars. To view death by looking at dead persons and thus see it for what it actually is seems unnecessary or even an intrusion on the privacy of the dead.

Looking at the dead is unseemly. Even if many consider the execution of some of the worst criminals as a necessity, very few advocate that it be done publicly. Recently the Pentagon worked extremely hard to keep even the photographs of the coffins of dead American soldiers from publication. And we

162

do not see the corpses of those who have died through sundry means on the evening news or in our daily papers. It would be too disturbing, so we usually see a photo of the victim taken while they were healthy and happy. It seems to be so much better for us that our knowledge and thoughts about death stay abstract and notional. Even the viewing of the dead at wakes is sanitized by mortuary science: the casket may be left open for us to view the body only if the dearly departed looks lifelike.

The more we push the reality of death away, the more we are simultaneously fascinated and drawn to fictionalized depictions of death on television, in the movies, and in video games. These illusory and sanitized views of death capture our imaginations, and we gravitate toward them, perhaps because they reinforce our hope that death is the ultimate unreality. It is perfectly all right for an actor to die bloodlessly on screen, because deep down we know that he is not really dead. And when a virtual person is slain in a video game, it takes very little for us to attempt to make the connection that death itself is only something virtual. Of course none of this is ever entirely convincing, but they seem to be the only ways we are willing to consider death—from a distance, far from our loved ones and us.

This way of looking at death as something idealized, sanitized, and fictionalized is akin to pornography and is perverse in the same way. The airbrushing of bodies devalues our physical selves, and fantasy sex devalues lovemaking; airbrushing death devalues our lives, and fantasy death devalues our dying. As pornography makes us blind to the beauty and blessedness of sex, so do the fantasized depictions of death make us blind to its beauty and blessedness.

Because we want to think with Gadamer that death is something incomprehensible, we prefer to view it from the perspective of the immortal. In fact, if Gadamer is right, then we can view it only from that perspective—as beings who can always anticipate a future in which we are participants. And if the prospect of death is too disturbing, or if we see the foolishness of the fictionalized depictions, then we can just change the channel and watch the immortal Lucy and Desi.

I Love Jesus functions much in the same way as *I Love Lucy*. It is less a palliative and more an anesthetic. I think we take scripture's rather frequent references to Jesus's triumph over death to mean that no one should ever die—especially me. Jesus died so I don't have to; and since I don't have to die, there's not much point in me considering it and being morbid or depressed. Certainly not always, but often enough our liturgies, religious gatherings, and talk about church stress the risen Christ of Easter Sunday and deemphasize or ignore the death and burial of Jesus the criminally subversive outcast. It is as though we prefer to think of Jesus only or exclusively as our triumphal Lord and close our eyes to his execution, as if his crucifixion is something unseemly, and as if the resurrection makes any sense without his preceding death.

Thus far what I have written, even in this abbreviated form, is a commonplace, at least for those who have spent some time reading and thinking about death. During my time of looking at death, it has occurred to me that I am rather more afraid of dying than I am of death itself—though perhaps I just cannot get beyond thoughts of my dying to reach a real consideration of my death itself. On my good days, I have studied enough Plato to think I can be philosophical about death: either it is nothing, or it is something. And I have just as much reason to think that death will be pleasant as I do to think that it will not. And when I take off the philosophical robes and consider that I am a child of God, my worries about what follows this life tend to dissipate. At least, as I've said, on my good days.

But dying is another matter entirely.

Even though it may not be much, I have seen just enough dying to know that sometimes it involves a great deal of pain and suffering. I worry more about that prospect than I do about death itself. To some small extent I understand how death can become an "arbitral reward" and why it can be looked forward to with eager anticipation and greeted with relief. It is that particular way of dying—the kind of dying that precedes death as a reward—which frightens me. I see myself suffering too much to moan, barely able to think (but to think enough to be self-aware), and unable to focus on anything but the pain. I worry about becoming only pain. And I worry about being so anesthetized by pain management that I fall to the other extreme: that I feel nothing, become nothing, and barely exist in some hazy demisleep.

Perhaps if I do not become nothing or only pain, then maybe my suffering will leave me so focused on myself that I will not be aware of the presence of those I love. And perhaps if the suffering is not quite that great, it will be so gruesome and sickening that my loved ones will not be able to bear watching, hearing, and smelling me die, so that I will find myself dying alone or with no one's hand to hold other than that of some doctor, nurse, or priest whose name I can't remember and whose face I won't be able to see clearly. These things matter to me now, and I worry that they will not matter to me then.

Well, those few paragraphs were uncomfortable to write, and I can imagine how they must read. They are, perhaps, the neurotic reflections of a person with too much time on his hands—at least, that thought occurs to me as I reread them. There is something about staying busy that keeps these anxieties at the furthest removes of our minds, because we do not like thinking about our own dying. Even if Gadamer is right that our deaths are incomprehensible, our dying is not. In fact, it seems so real that with any fatigue or discomfort I feel, I wonder if it might be the beginning of the dying. But even with all this said, what concerns me more right now is not the basic fear I think we all have when we contemplate our dying, but more of the spiritual anxiety that comes over us as believers who face dying. As though the two are separable.

St. John writes about the resurrection of Lazarus in the eleventh chapter of his Gospel narrative. While the calling of Lazarus back from the dead is illustrative of God's power and mercy, there is another aspect of the story that also deserves our attention. Jesus is summoned by Martha and Mary while Lazarus is ill, yet he does not go to them until Lazarus has been in the tomb for four days. Jesus waits. He explains (11:4) that the result of Lazarus's illness will be for God's glory—that Lazarus's death will serve as an object lesson for all believers.

Yet neither Martha nor Mary know of this explanation for Jesus's lateness. What they do know is that they have called for their friend who they know can save their brother—and he did not come, he did not respond, he did not even send a message. When the sisters hear that Jesus finally is coming, their reaction to the news is very different. Martha leaves their house, where they are grieving, and goes to meet Jesus with eagerness. When she reaches him she says, "Lord, if you had been here, my brother would not have died, but even now I know that God will grant whatever you ask of him" (11:21–22). In her actions—leaving her house and her mourning—and also by her words, Martha professes her faith in the power and mercy of the Lord.

On the other hand, Mary did not leave the house when she heard that Jesus had arrived; she stayed where she was and remained in her quiet mourning. In fact, Mary needed a special invitation to come out: it was only when Martha called to her and said that Jesus wanted to see her that Mary finally got up to meet him. When she reached him, "she threw herself at his feet, saying, 'Lord, if you had been here, my brother would not have died'" (11:32). While the evangelist does not indicate what Mary's tone of voice was, it is significant that she repeats only the first half of Martha's statement to the Lord. Mary makes no profession of faith, she speaks only from her mourning, and, I think, her words reproach Jesus for his lateness and apparent indifference. Neither Martha nor Mary were aware of Jesus's stated reasons for his delay at 11:4, and I think we should read Mary's response as from one who feels betrayed—angry and hurt—just as we should read Martha's response as a trusting one.

Immediately following Mary's confrontation with Jesus, the Gospel tells us that Jesus was distressed at the sight of her grief. At verse 35, which I am told is the shortest verse in scripture, John writes, "Jesus wept."

Why was Jesus distressed? Why did Jesus weep? The reaction of the crowd that John reports is clearly incorrect. When the Jews saw Jesus weeping they said, "See how much he loved him!" But Jesus could not have been weeping for his friend Lazarus. Jesus already knew Lazarus was dead, if not while he waited in Jerusalem before responding to the sisters' summons, then certainly by the time he arrived in Bethany. Nor did Jesus weep because his dear friends were grieving. Again, if he did not know beforehand that the sisters would be grief-stricken, he could certainly see when he arrived that Martha was grieving, and he obviously was not distressed when he met with her and saw her face and her reaction to her brother's death. None of these elements explains why Jesus became distressed and wept when he did.

Jesus weeps only after he sees Mary and hears how little she has to say to him. Jesus weeps because Mary's faith is shattered. She makes no profession of belief in his power and mercy, nor does she proclaim his goodness and closeness to the Father—perhaps because she no longer believes any of it. She does not assent—as Martha does—to Jesus's teaching "I am the Resurrection" (11:25), because Jesus does not even attempt to tell it to her. Even though Mary's statement to Jesus echoes Martha's, Mary's "if you had been here, my brother would not have died" is a slap at Jesus for what she sees as his nonresponsiveness and callous disregard for Lazarus's suffering. Jesus feels the pain of that rebuke and recognizes how badly harmed Mary is. His only response to her at that time is to weep, because he has no words to say to her. He proceeds to the tomb and raises Lazarus, demonstrating the power he has over death and illustrating his teaching that whoever believes in him, even though that person dies, will live.

This story speaks to my fear of dying and the spiritual anxiety that the fear brings. When they were confronted with Lazarus's dying, both Mary and Martha responded with hope born of their faith in Jesus. They called to him and summoned him to relieve the pain and suffering and save their brother from death. Their belief was that Jesus would respond; they had based their hope for Lazarus's salvation upon it. But Jesus did not come in time. He did not respond in a manner they could recognize, and he did not act in the way they asked, and what he did do was for reasons about which they were ignorant. Even though her hope was apparently frustrated, Martha maintained her faith in the lordship and goodness of Jesus; her hope for Lazarus's cure became transformed into a hope for something else because of that faith. With Mary, on the other hand, a different kind of transformation took place. Somewhere along this pathway, Mary's hope that Jesus would cure Lazarus and save him from death became more fundamental than her faith. In fact, her faith became dependent on that particular and specific hope. When that hope was frustrated by Jesus's failure to respond in the way he was asked, and Lazarus therefore died, Mary's faith was damaged so much that she did not even react on her own initiative to Jesus's coming to see her. She needed to be called out by her sister, the one who was deeply connected to her by sharing most fully in her grief.

My anxiety is that when I am dying my hope will supplant my faith the way Mary's did. I will bargain, cajole, and plead, and I know even now that the Lord will not respond to my summons in the way I expect or fulfill my hope the way I want. I will die. And I pray that I will die like Martha and not like Mary.

The story of Lazarus is not only about Lazarus being dead; it is also about Mary dying. Jesus did not have to raise Lazarus from the dead for Martha to maintain her faith, but I am not so sure the same could be said for Mary. Mary, it seems, needed the miracle Jesus performed in order for her faith to be brought back to life. The power over death that Jesus has is the power not only over our bodies' dying but also over our souls' dying. His resurrection of Lazarus's body is also—and even more importantly—a resurrection of Mary. "Whoever lives and believes in me will never die" (11:26). By bringing her belief in him back to her, Jesus rescues Mary from death in the same way that Lazarus responds to his call. I know that I will summon Jesus to save me when I am dying, and I hope we both will know clearly what is to be saved when I make that summons.

So this is, I believe, the fundamental difficulty of the last chapter. Our call to follow Jesus and be peacemakers means that we will die. We don't like this message, so we recoil from it and consider it incomprehensible; and we find ways to try to reinterpret the gospel or to understand the "real" meaning of Jesus's message in order to obfuscate and avoid this conclusion. He could not have meant what he said; "death" must be a metaphor for something else.

We maneuver in this way because we are afraid. The anxiety of dying and death—in their physical and spiritual manifestations—seems overwhelming in their incomprehensibility. We are already on Mary's path in the Lazarus story. Our relationship to Jesus has become inverted in that our hope is more fundamental than our faith, and our expectations of him determine how we will live; rather, we ought to understand that his expectations of us should determine how we will die.

There is another difficulty with that preceding chapter, a difficulty that is not as fundamental as the Marian inversion I have just discussed above, but still an important one. In fact, I think that the two difficulties are related to each other in an integral way.

Peacemaking and death as a response to the Hitler question strikes us as implausible if not incomprehensible also because it seems so radical and extreme. Whenever I have been asked the Hitler question and whenever I have heard other pacifists asked it, the question always posits that the Holocaust is under way. We are placed in the middle of the German Reich and are asked what we will do now. The question invariably plunks us down into a situation of facing the evil that Hitler represents all of a sudden, and the only options that appear open to us are to acquiesce to the evil, kill the evildoers, or die. I think our tendency is to recoil at the starkness of the choices: we are confronted with a terrible dilemma in the situation because the first two of our choices have something significant to recommend them. Killing the evildoers eliminates the threat and saves some innocents; acquiescence promotes our own survival, which seems to be a law of nature. The third choice, on the other hand, appears to come from left field and does not seem to be a response at all. How can we be expected to be peacemakers and repay evil with good in these circumstances? Peacemaking here in the Reich looks like an armchair philosophical or theological reaction to a real-world problem, and, as such, it places on Christians an unrealistic expectation that is above and beyond what the gospel requires of us. In other words, the answer contained in the last chapter is implausible precisely because it is so far removed from our experience and what we intuitively think we ought to do as the church, and also because it seems so extreme in what it says the gospel means for us in a concrete application. The answer is outrageous in its extraordinariness.

I think this difficulty is right on the mark. As long as peacemaking and repaying evil with good are seen as extraordinary, they will also be seen as outrageous. I think this is also true for most of what the gospel calls us to be as disciples of the Lord: the prohibitions against divorce and fornication, the requirement to give of our goods and ourselves to the poor, that we must love all our neighbors—even the bad ones—and on and on. All of these things run contrary to our instinctive reactions; all of them are unnatural; all of them are counterintuitive; and all of them appear extraordinary. And in the right circumstances—circumstances that occur too often—they are also outrageous. We have a problem with the message of the gospel, but the problem is with us and not with the message itself. Our task as the church is not simply to grit our teeth and accept peacemaking as the outrageous requirement it appears to be but to live lives of following Jesus in such a way that such actions (they are all related to each other) become ordinary and run-of-the-mill, so that they express the way we *are* as people of God.

In a very important respect, the Hitler question is a dishonest one, or at the very least misleading. It assumes that Christians and the church have no involvement and no responsibility prior to some arbitrary date in the early 1940s. If the question is asking how a pacifistic church should have responded to the horrors of the Holocaust, the answer surely lies in being a peacemaking church long before the Holocaust ever began. The church should have preached and lived a love of the Jews for many centuries before the twentieth; the church should have formed Christians into the kind of people who do not kill Jews, or homosexuals, or gypsies, or communists, or other Christians, or Nazis, or whoever else was victimized by the war. The church should have lived and taught in such a way that the First World War would have been incomprehensible in a largely Christian Europe and, failing that, should have railed against the Versailles Treaty and the vengeance it embodied in favor of forgiveness and reconciliation. The failure of the church and of Christians to be peacemakers in 1942 is horrible precisely because it is a result and culmination of centuries of failure. Antisemitism, violence, warfare, strife, hatred, and intolerance have been and continue to be acceptable practices for Christians—usually in the name of politics, nationalism, or even religious truth. This is how it has been for so long that Hannah Arendt's insight should not be surprising—that the evil of the Holocaust can be viewed as something banal.

It is a sad but common exercise to point an accusatory finger at the church for its centuries of failure and what appears to be its willful refusal to live the gospel, its rejection of its responsibility to teach discipleship. It is also sad, often heart-wrenching, and certainly less common to point an accusatory finger at individual Christians like Dietrich Bonhoeffer. Accusing not only those who supported Hitler but also those who acquiesced as well as those who engaged in brutalizing violence for their failures, their evil acts, and their misguided responses, all as contrary to the gospel, gives me very strong reason to pause.

As I write this book and especially this chapter, I notice a triumphal melody lurking in the background. It is the same type of arrogant hypocrisy that Orwell noticed in the pacifists he addressed during the Second World War in Britain. It is not clear to me that as a church we are, and as a Christian I am, any better peacemakers than our brothers and sisters of that time and place. Genocides still occur: witness Bosnia, Rwanda, and Darfur. Wars are still waged. And while we profess our adherence to the message of the gospel, we (at least in the North American church) are still preoccupied with our personal concerns, with our security, and with whether more dioceses will declare bankruptcy. We seem to consider many of the horrible events around us to be abstract geopolitical issues, if we consider them at all. We have no reason to be smug or confident or to indulge in a sense of moral superiority toward those who have gone before us. On the contrary, we may be in even worse shape than they were, because we have their example to learn from. We therefore appear to be doubly blind: we have not learned from them, and we are just as frightened of dying and lacking in faith as they were.

So the question that remains to be answered is how we, as a community of disciples, can learn to follow the path that Jesus shows us and become peacemakers, especially when making peace may lead to our death. The initial response is, I think, fairly obvious.

First of all we must grow stronger in faith so that we can react to dying and death more like Martha. Our faith provides the foundation and context for who we are and what we are called to do. Without the recognition and grounding of the kingdom we are called to serve, loving sacrifice and forgiveness become morbidly naive in the face of secular geopolitical "realities." Without faith, physical death becomes what we fear most and try hardest to avoid; death retains its frightful mystery and power over us. Death becomes a god who demands obeisance and burnt offerings.

Second, we have to become peacemakers in all aspects of our lives in the way the gospel teaches. At base, we are called to be saints, but sainthood is not really about the canonization process or even recognition by the church community. Rather, the saints of the church are those who live their lives in the way we have been taught. In the context of this book it may seem that I am urging on all of us a heroic martyrdom, but the reality is much simpler. Our call to be peacemakers is a call to make peace and carry Christ with us, particularly in our mundane activities and interactions. Recalling Levinas, we must avoid violence in all its forms. The way the Christian response to the Hitler question becomes comprehensible and loses its extraordinary character is only by its being congruent with the way we always act.

To sum up, then, the main difficulty in accepting the implications of our call to be peacemakers is our fear of death and dying, born of a weakness of faith. By strengthening our faith and remaining open to God's grace through the everyday practice of our discipleship, we can become schooled in what it means to bring the light to all people.

Ninth Meditation

2 Corinthians 4:7–12; 5:14–18

But we hold this treasure in pots of earthenware, so that the immensity of the power is God's and not our own. We are subjected to every kind of hardship, but never distressed; we see no way out but we never despair; we are pursued but never cut off; knocked down, but still have some life in us; always we carry with us in our body the death of Jesus so that the life of Jesus, too, may be visible in our body. Indeed, while we are still alive, we are continually being handed over to death, for the sake of Jesus, so that the life of Jesus, too, may be visible in our mortal flesh. In us, then, death is at work; in you, life. . . .

For the love of Christ overwhelms us when we consider that if one man died for all, then all have died; his purpose in dying for all humanity was that those who live should live not any more for themselves, but for him who died and was raised to life for them.

From now onwards, then, we will not consider anyone by human standards: even if we were once familiar with Christ according to human standards, we do not know him in that way any longer. So for anyone who is in Christ, there is a new creation: the old order is gone and a new being is there to see. It is all God's work; he reconciled us to himself through Christ and he gave us the ministry of reconciliation.

■ Lord, help me to remember that I am always in your presence.

I feel like an earthenware pot, though an empty and dry one. This book is wearing heavily on me, Lord. I don't want to pray in public anymore, my prologue stories remind me of all my failures, and there is no joy in the rest

171

of it. I can understand why there would be very little happiness in a book about Hitler and the evil he represents, but I don't know how to communicate the joy that runs through all the things you call us to be and do.

Paul is able to capture this joy in a very subtle way. He points to it when he says we see no way out yet we never despair. But I often see a way out: I have just enough talent to convince myself that what I want to do is consistent with your word, but not enough talent to really believe it; so I end up in a place that is awfully close to despair. I struggle an awful lot with what I believe is inevitable and in such a way that, whatever I do, I'm miserable.

I don't see how your life is made visible in my body—even though I am conscious of carrying your death with me. In the last chapter I wrote about our tendency to focus on your resurrection at the expense of your passion, and I fear I have gone too far the other way and have lost all feeling for and sight of Easter.

Paul again seems to indicate a way to connect the two that often eludes me. The passion is not separable from the resurrection. I think that's why Paul says that your love overwhelms us when we consider your death. I am sorry to say that it is only on rare occasions that I can look at your death and explore what it means in a way that does not abstract either your death or its meaning beyond its real significance. I find it difficult not to abstract too much: so often I find myself living only in my mind, walking among ideas and concepts. I mean, it's easy for me to attribute what you have done to your love for me, but it's very hard for me to understand what that love is.

I think that part of my problem is that "considering" love pulls me away from love, much as considering humor pulls me away from what is funny. When I consider love, it becomes an abstract and lifeless thing, like a desiccated and dissected corpse. And while it might be valuable to dissect a body to understand the physical parts of life, we need to remember that we are really looking at what is dead. When we think of love and examine its parts (indeed, if it has parts) and what those parts imply, we need also to remember the similar inertness of our concepts and their distance from us and the life we live. Too often I delude myself by believing that the ideas I think about in the quiet of my study are exactly the same as the things they represent, and that my mastery of the inert concept gives me mastery of the dynamic object.

So how do I understand your love and when am I overwhelmed by it? If I look at what is more familiar, I know I am overwhelmed by my wife's love for me only when I hold her love for me while, at the same time, I also see myself truthfully. It is in this simultaneous consideration of those two facts that I am overwhelmed, because only then do I recognize deeply that her love for me is pure gift—that I have done nothing to deserve it. And through that gift she gives me, I become a better man than I could on my own.

Perhaps that is what I need to do with you. As my wife's love makes me a better man and more worthy of her love, so does your love and sacrifice transform me. And since you give your love to all, everyone is transformed, and through that transformation I can see the new creation by your standards, through your eyes. You know exactly what we are in our weakness and frailty—empty pots of clay. It is only through your filling of us that even the ugliest and meanest of pots becomes a valuable vessel, even when we can't *see* on our own that the pot contains anything at all. To see the new order, the new being that exists in each of us, that is what you call us to do.

Here is the joy that is born of our faith, and here is the joy that underlies the hardship and distress. Your love for us is what makes all of us worthy of love. To deny it for anyone is to deny it for myself; to affirm it for everyone is also to affirm it for myself. Our undeserving transformation into worthwhile beings, what we are called to be and to do for each other, how we must reconcile and be reconciled, it is all your work.

Bless my mind to illuminate me with your wisdom;
bless my lips to allow me speak your word;
and bless my heart that I might live the gospel.

9

Elaborating upon the Elaboration

Prologue

In late 1980 or thereabout, I was working part-time on the night shift in a diner in Queens, New York. It was just what I needed at the time, because I had lost my "real" job and the health insurance that went with it sometime before when I was diagnosed with leukemia. Through the kindness of the doctors at the hospital, I was treated as an indigent John Doe, which wasn't far from true. When I wasn't worrying that I would end up in a hospital ward being cared for by some Cancer Care Technician who didn't even know how to change bedsheets, I slept during the day; whenever I was able, I would walk the streets at night, and when I wasn't able, I'd watch old movies on television. Money and food were scarce, so when I went into remission I was so painfully thin that I think the owner of the diner took mercy on me: she gave me a job and allowed me to eat as much as I could hold.

One night near midnight during my break, a fellow came in and sat next to me at the counter and ordered a cup of coffee. He looked over at the two platters (one of meat loaf, the other with mashed potatoes) that were in front of me, laughed, and asked where I put it. I just smiled and nodded. I was never what anyone would describe as a friendly person, and since I had cut myself off from friends and family when I had gotten sick, I wasn't used to being around people or talking much.

He was oblivious to my attempts to ignore him and continued to chatter on and on. He told me his name was Tim, that he was originally from Nebraska, of all places, and had just come to New York to be a playwright. He was telling me much more than I wanted to know, but he did it in such a captivating way that he not only held my interest but also made me almost believe that he could be a playwright. Even though he was clearly a hayseed of the first order, there was something about his openness that was so uncommonly innocent that I felt an urge to take care of him. I asked for my usual two pieces of pie and gave him one. Murray the cook gave me a dirty look: he wasn't too pleased about feeding me, and now I was giving his pie to some goniff off the street. Besides, I had just killed whatever slim chance he had of getting a decent tip.

Tim ate it in a way that told me it had been some time since he had eaten pie, and while he ate I looked him over. I noticed that his clothes were clean but very worn. He was also wearing an incredibly elaborate pair of cowboy boots.

"Nice boots, Tim."

"Yes, you think so too? They're a little big but the most comfortable things I've ever worn." He lit a cigarette, sipped some coffee, and ate a forkful of pie simultaneously.

"You get them in Nebraska?"

"No, no. Here in New York. They're a dead man's boots."

I didn't want to ask, and suddenly he wasn't talking, so I figured he wanted me to ask. There are times when curiosity overwhelms stubbornness, so I finally did ask what the story was. Tim smiled victoriously and told me that he was a priest. He was on leave from his religious order because, among other reasons, they didn't want him to write plays—well, at least not in New York. But he came anyway and was living in some flophouse in Brooklyn. A neighbor there was dying, and Tim gave him last rites. The dying man expressed concern about his funeral, because he had no money. Tim told him not to worry, that he would make sure it was a grand funeral—incense and all. The dying man gave Tim his boots. Tim shrugged. "I couldn't say no. He was a mean guy; these boots were his treasure, and not to take them would be to keep him from making the only gift of thanks he could. I still think of them as his boots; I just wear them."

A playwright priest wearing a dead man's boots. I liked this guy.

Over the next couple of weeks Tim came by often for coffee and pie, and he'd walk me to the train when my shift was over. I finally asked him if he would hear my confession. It had been a while, and I felt a need to get straight with God.

He said that he would hear my confession. For all that I thought Tim was a corn-fed yokel, never before or since have I met someone who could read a soul half as well. While he was gentle, his honesty felt brutal, and he brought me to be brutally honest with myself. When I was finished, he told me that I really should have said that I thought God needed to get straight with me. I didn't understand right away, but as we talked it became clear: Tim told me I had turned Jonathan Edwards on his head in that God was in the hands of an angry sinner. God had not abandoned me as I thought, living my days (as I was then) through some of the Psalms, but I had abandoned him. I don't know how long that confession lasted, because Tim made me take off my watch before we started, but eventually came the penance. I wasn't expecting any of this.

"For your penance, Bob, I want you to go dancing."

"Huh?"

"Dancing. You know, with your arms around a woman, moving together to music? It's called 'fun.'"

"That's the stupidest penance I've ever heard."

"Oh, yeah. You would prefer me to tell you to go off and put pebbles in your shoes, or pray for forty hours on your knees. But that stuff's an abomination. Reconciliation everywhere else is a time of joy, and this now is a time of joy for both you and God. You have to treat it that way."

"But I'm not dating anyone. I don't even know a woman."

"Come on. What about that brunette waitress in the diner?"

"Eva Hernandez? You've got to be kidding. She'd kill me."

"I'm not telling you to sleep with her. Just go dancing. She looks like she might know some good clubs."

"I'm not talking about sleeping with her, you, you priest. Listen, if she ever found out that I went out with her as a penance, first she'd gut me and then she'd come after you, and she won't buy any of your cockamamie theology either."

So we argued about it a while longer, and he finally relented. He decided that for my penance I had to take Murray out to dinner: wine, dessert, the whole smack. Tim figured that since Murray had been feeding me, it was about time that I fed him. He actually thought highly of Murray! We embraced and I went home feeling better than I had in a very long time, whole. I never told Tim, but that dinner with Murray was more like a traditional penance, like praying with pebbles under my knees for forty hours.

I saw Tim a lot after that. It was similar to hanging out with a not particularly precocious seven-year-old. We went to the zoo, where he was captivated by the monkeys—I walked away when he tried (without any success by my lights) to communicate with them. He tried to teach me to finger-paint, but I told him he was nuts and would have none of it. And he went into a delighted frenzy making blue snakes and little people when he found a container of Play Doh someplace. When I tried to be more adult and talk to him about politics and Marx, it took me twenty minutes to realize he was making connections to Zeppo, whom Tim regarded as an underappreciated comic master. He was simultaneously absurd and intriguing, magnetic and startling. He would start what would turn out to be long conversations with random strangers, Wall Streeters as well as street people, and almost always left them laughing.

I'll never understand how, but he managed to get one of his plays staged in a small community theater in, of all places, Larchmont—a tiny suburb in Westchester County. I went to the opening night as well as the cast party afterward. Tim had taken care of the refreshments: two gallons of muscatel and a couple of trays of peanut butter and jelly sandwiches. Raspberry, no less, because "raspberry jelly goes better with the wine than marmalade." Oddly true, but beside the point. Anyway, the local paper's reviewer liked the play about as much as the cast liked the refreshments: he hated it and, I'm sorry to say, he was right. That play was a dreadful thing to endure.

Tim was disappointed, of course. We were having coffee a few days later, and I asked him if he had another play to try out or if he'd go back to Nebraska since his playwriting had seemed to fail. He said that he didn't know what he would do next, but he wouldn't be going back to Nebraska and his religious order in any case. The other reason that he had left and come to New York was that he was gay.

This revelation changed something. I had never thought of Tim as a sexual person, so I can't really say that finding out he was gay was a surprise or had any impact on that score. And I had never thought of myself as homophobic—or racist or sexist or in any way intolerant, for that matter. Intellectually I knew that Tim's homosexuality didn't make any difference, yet there seemed to be some part of me that it did make a difference to. Those were the days before I admitted just how deeply bourgeois I am, and before gays were a recognized part of the bourgeois lifestyle.

Suddenly I became tense and jittery sitting next to him at the counter, and even though I didn't say anything to him about it, I had a hunch he noticed the change in the atmosphere, in me. But even if he was oblivious to my change in attitude then, he surely knew I was bothered when I avoided our customary embrace as I left for home. He stopped coming by the diner, and I didn't see him for a considerable time.

As is usual with me and unpleasantness, I tried not to think about it, but the whole episode kept replaying itself in my mind as I tried to get to sleep. Cognitively I knew it shouldn't make any difference; Tim was the same as he had always been, and I didn't know why his revelation had affected me the way it had. More: he had just experienced a major disappointment and, perhaps for the first time, needed my help and support. It took a while for me to admit finally that I was revulsed by my reaction and the way I was treating someone who was my friend and one who had tried to teach me so much about the gospel. I was ashamed I had learned so little. And the more time passed, the harder it became for me to face him.

It wasn't a conscious decision, so I'm not sure how it happened or in what way my will might have been involved, but one evening I found myself in a liquor store near where he lived. I bought a bottle of muscatel and climbed the stairs to his room. I knocked on the door, mostly hoping that he was out.

He grinned when he opened the door and saw me, took the bottle and squealed, "Great timing! I have jelly donuts!" and ushered me in as though he had just seen me the day before. He was chattering away about some new project when I had to stop him. I asked him to hear my confession. When I asked him for his own forgiveness, he just smiled and said, "489 to go." I was in my usual state of puzzlement until he reminded me about seventy times seven. For my penance he opened the box of jelly donuts and the bottle of wine, and we finger-painted our favorite scenes of Prospect Park in Brooklyn.

As we sat there laughing, painting, and not noticing how bad jelly donuts taste when covered in finger-paint, I thanked him for being home, because I didn't know how well I could have borne the burden if he weren't there to forgive me. He stopped and grew quiet. Finally he said that he had often prayed over our obligation to forgive one another but had never thought about our obligation to be available to receive the grace of an apology. "God waits for sinners, so perhaps we should wait for each other as well." At the end of the night we embraced, and I went home.

About a week later I received a package. Tim was on his way back to Nebraska, and he had sent me his boots.

———※———

■ At the end of the last chapter I attempted to answer the question of how we can learn to become peacemakers in the manner of Jesus, especially when that may lead us to our death. The answer I gave came in two parts: we need to grow stronger in faith, and we also need to become peacemakers in all aspects of our lives, especially the mundane. In short, we need to live the way the gospel teaches us on a daily basis.

Knowing where we need to end up is easy; figuring out precisely how to get there is another matter entirely. I have no doubt that there are many ways for us to deepen our faith and live lives of peace, but the path I wish to suggest is one delineated by the spiritual and corporal works of mercy. It is vitally important, though, to stress that the most essential foundation for this pathway—as for any of the other pathways we pursue—is prayer.

The centrality of prayer for the life of Christians is, once again, hardly a novel notion; it is a prescription that all of us have heard many times before, perhaps so often that we think we know what it means. Our tradition is replete with different ways to pray and modes of prayer; one need only to look at the shelves of spirituality sections of bookstores or at Amazon.com. Like diets, ways of praying come in and out of fashion as the centuries or even decades progress, and it is fairly easy to find a method that suits our individual taste if we have a mind to look and explore, or even ask someone we respect to serve as a mentor. What I am concerned with and what I believe is necessary has very little to do with the specific methodology of how we should pray.

As I read scripture and contemplate what it has to say about prayer, I am at first comforted by the simplicity. To go into just a couple of examples from Matthew's Gospel, at 6:5–15 Jesus cautions us to pray quietly and not to "babble as the gentiles do, for they think that by using many words they will make themselves heard."

In the example of prayer that he gives us, the major elements of our discipleship appear and are emphasized. In the first place, we should call upon the Father and bless his name, acknowledging him as One and Lord. Second, we pray that his kingdom come and that his will be worked, and that both of these occur on earth at this moment. By these two movements we assent to our dependency on him as well as his lordship, and we accept the working of his grace through us in bringing the kingdom to fruition and completeness.

We ask for bread and forgiveness, the things that sustain us in our fellowship with one another and with God, and without which we would starve, consumed by our hunger, our desires, our selves. What sustains us is, of course, not bread alone but also the Word of God acting through us. In this prayer of Jesus we call on God to forgive us as we have forgiven, and at the end of the passage (14–15) Jesus makes this explicit: "Yes, if you forgive others their failings, your heavenly Father will forgive you yours; but if you do not forgive others, your Father will not forgive your failings either." Apparently our prayer is to remind us of the symmetry of mercy: our practice of mercy indicates to God that his kingdom has come and his will is being done. Our prayer reminds us that by being merciful we will receive mercy.

Yet there are other passages about prayer that puzzle me so much that I have often wondered if they should be taken at all literally. In many ways they are like what have become known as the "hard sayings" of the gospel. The hard sayings are the commands or prescriptions that are very difficult for disciples to follow, and I have spoken about some of them throughout this book. The hard sayings call us to behave in ways that don't seem natural to us—turning the other cheek, giving our shirt also when only our cloak is asked for . . . things like that. But there are other sayings that don't seem to get the press the hard sayings do, probably because they go beyond hard. These sayings cross over the borderland of being merely very difficult and into very troublesome territory. The first group of these that I wish to discuss a little bit are contained in three Pauline letters and pertain directly to prayer.

In Colossians 4:2, Paul writes, "Be persevering in your prayers and be thankful as you stay awake to pray." In the Letter to the Ephesians Paul makes two important references to prayer. At 5:19–20 he writes, "Sing psalms and hymns and inspired songs among yourselves, singing and chanting to the Lord in your hearts, *always and everywhere giving thanks to God* who is our Father in the name of our Lord Jesus Christ" (emphasis here and below is added). Later in the letter, Paul reinforces this direction when he writes (6:18), "In all your prayer and entreaty *keep praying in the Spirit on every possible occasion.* Never get tired of staying awake to pray for all God's holy people. . . ." Finally, in 1 Thessalonians 5:15–18, Paul teaches, "Make sure that people do not try to repay evil for evil; always aim at what is best for each other and for everyone.

Always be joyful; pray constantly; and for all things give thanks; this is the will of God for you in Christ Jesus."

I think that initially it is not easy to know what to make of these teachings—and we should note that even my calling them "teachings" makes certain presumptions. Throughout our tradition and history we have taken these passages and softened them to "teachings" or recommendations or even as statements of idealized spirituality. When someone calls them "teachings" the implication is that they can be ignored or not taken all that seriously, like the teachings of college professors. When I say we have softened them to a status of idealized spirituality, I mean that we interpret them as pointing to some unattainable state. Who can realistically expect us to pray constantly and on every possible occasion?

While the question is rhetorical in intent, I believe that there is a clear answer: God expects us to. Surprisingly again, the gospel means exactly what it says. No amount of softening or interpretation that weakens these sayings is appropriate, nor can we hide behind notions of cultural or historical differences between ourselves and the early church to whom Paul wrote. Prayer needs to be so central, guiding, and consuming that we should do it constantly.

Nonetheless, we are very busy people. I doubt that we are any busier than the Ephesians or Thessalonians were; they too had to work, eat, play, and deal with all sorts of responsibilities. But even if we are so similar to those communities, the fact remains that the command to pray always appears to be an impossible one.

I am no guru of prayer, nor am I one who has obeyed this command and manages to pray constantly—let alone be always joyful. But where I think I may differ from many in the church is that I believe that it is possible to do so. I do not believe we are commanded to do things we cannot do or are called to be the kind of people we are not able to be. What I can offer here are a few reflections on why I think I have failed to live this command and outline some strategies that may help.

I have most often failed to pray because I am so busy. It is only partly a joke that I am so busy I don't know what I have actually accomplished in the course of a day. But even during most inventories of what I have done, prayer seems to be totally absent, let alone inconstant. It often seems impossible for me to fit my prayers into my active life, even when I am well intentioned and try to make sufficient plans and time for them. It occurs to me, though, that this is the wrong way to think, primarily because it messes up my priorities. Rather than trying to fit prayer into my busy schedule, perhaps what I should rather do is fit my schedule into my busy prayer life. It would make a significant difference if I no longer considered who I am by what job I have, what responsibilities consume me, and what roles I fulfill throughout the day, but rather understood who I am by whose I am. If I belong first and most completely to God, and if my prayer is the way I stay connected to him and maintain my belonging, then I need to schedule whatever else I do around that primary, identifying, and grounding relationship.

The second big mistake I commonly make is that I formalize my prayer too much. This error is related to the first and is implied throughout the preceding paragraph. I regard prayer as something that I do, that I have to arrange, whose conditions I have to set so that everything is just right and conducive to a spiritual communion I also idealize. I frequently think that if my prayer does not have a particular form and structure, or if the physical conditions of prayer—that I be free of distractions, in a comfortable room, etc.—are not optimal or how I prefer them, or if I do not realize a particular feeling of peace or sense the presence of the Lord, then my prayer is a failure. I become so distracted by structure, setting, and expectations of results that I completely miss the point. Perhaps I need to adjust my thinking again so I realize that prayer is not something that I do but rather something that happens to me.

Though I have trouble understanding what it means, we believe that God is always present. If that is so, then clearly I am always in his presence. Let me pursue an analogy. It strikes me that the times I have been closest to my wife (whether I felt it or not) have been those times when we have been together for large stretches of time, when we have grown so accustomed to having the other around that there was no novelty in being together. During those times it is never necessary to schedule "appointments" to catch up, or to plan elaborate dates like candlelit dinners, as we need to do when job and other responsibilities consume us. By being together and aware of the other's presence, we are able to be connected and grow together. In fact, it takes very little effort, and it doesn't much matter where we are or what, if anything, we happen to be doing. God's presence does more than half the work as well. Prayer need not be only a formal communication with the Almighty; the conscious awareness that we are in his presence is a beautiful prayer in itself that both humbles and exalts us. If the phrase I have often heard—that we must endeavor to make our lives a prayer—has any meaning, this might come close. But I must stress the point that we need to pray, especially in this way, with intentionality and consciousness. Though I have often heard it said that we must make our lives a prayer, it too often struck me as a way to justify not praying. Prayer does not seem to mean anything without the fundamental consciousness of God's presence and our intention to be with him.

The best way I have found to maintain this consciousness and intention in my usual distracted state is by periodically engaging in formulaic prayer.

When I am tired or busy or distressed, it is easier for me to use the language and forms of our tradition. In addition, adhering to a discipline of formulaic or prescribed prayer keeps me grounded. Sometimes I am able to move beyond my own selfish relationship with God and beyond a focus on my own concerns or interests or fears and connect more concretely with the church and the people of God. One of the more fruitful ways I have found to do this is by praying the Liturgy of the Hours. By praying the prayers of the church at a number of prescribed times during the day, I find the language and heart of the church and its tradition. I am able to locate myself within the community and can see that my connection with the church is one that spans millennia. There is something about praying an ancient prayer or singing an old hymn that draws us closer to the saints that precede us as well as to the saints who will follow: we pray the same and are nurtured the same.

The connection we have with one another through time is a crucial one; the church is called "the body of Christ" for a reason. It is important for faithful discipleship that we leave behind the mythic notions of individuality that foster beliefs that we are independent and self-sufficient, solitary and set apart from others around us. In what it requires of us and in the picture of discipleship it describes, the gospel is the antithesis of individuality. The times that I have found myself in a constant state of prayer for days were those times when I was totally dependent on the will of God, during the serious illness of loved ones. It seemed as if every breath I took included a supplication to him and as though the beating of my heart was prayer when my mind was too overwhelmed to speak. The remarkable thing is not that I was so dependent on God's grace during those times, but that I do not see that I am equally dependent on him even when I feel strong and in control. To be able to pray constantly requires this deep sense of reliance and subordination. Further, I find myself unable to do this alone. I cannot see myself as dependent on God through an act of my own will, nor should I wait for a moment of necessity to establish this right relation. I need to open myself to it as a member of a community of the faithful.

The only way we can begin to move away from the hypocrisy that Orwell and Bonhoeffer indict us for is by engaging in those practices that bring us together in recognition of our dependence on God, a dependency that moves beyond the self and into communal fellowship with all of his people. We need to worship together not only because Jesus taught us to but also because it is a necessary element to our acceptance of our connection with each other as the church and the whole people of God. We need the support and example that others provide, and we need an antidote to the poisonous lie that I am able to be a disciple alone. We need to come together in the presence of the Lord to recognize that his saving grace is meant for all. We need to pray together so that we can teach and support one another in prayer and in our work as disciples, and we must come to know each other in these ways so that we can hold each other accountable. Not surprisingly, it is easier for me to hide and to tell myself the lies I want to hear when I am alone than when I am with others. When I am with others who know me, I can be held to a higher standard than I usually hold myself, can be called in specific instances to be truthful and kind, and can experience the forgiveness and reconciliation I need, which binds me to my brothers and sisters. In other words, I am less likely to be a jerk or act like a selfish fool around people who know my name and have no fear of speaking the truth. This is one of the blessings of my family—that they can puncture my pretensions, call me to be a better person, and do it all in an atmosphere of love. The body of Christ can be the same blessing with regular contact and disciplined worship.

Thus far I have outlined some of the difficulties to prayer that I have experienced and a few suggestions for improving our relation with God. Although I have written that prayer is the most important and basic foundation for who we are, we must also include the other aspects of the pathway to discipleship and living faithfully, the spiritual and corporal works of mercy.

Because I am saying that our answer as peacemaking Christians to the Hitler question is so difficult that it appears incomprehensible without a thorough-going preparation, prayer is not enough. Through our everyday and common practices we must form ourselves into the kind of people who behave as peacemakers, who live lives of disciples not only in our hearts and souls but also through the expression of our actions. It is only when violence in all aspects of our lives—especially those that seem trivial—becomes incomprehensible that peacemaking and love will show themselves to us as being the "natural" responses to evil. Through daily acts of mercy we need to habituate ourselves to be the people of God.

The works of mercy are the ancient way the church has developed of making the required actions of discipleship more concrete; they are culled from various aspects of scripture—especially the Beatitudes and the Sermon on the Mount—as well as from our long tradition.

The Spiritual Works of Mercy

- Instructing
- Advising
- Consoling
- Comforting

- Bearing wrongs patiently
- Forgiving

The Corporal Works of Mercy

- Feeding the hungry
- Sheltering the homeless
- Clothing the naked
- Giving alms to the poor
- Visiting the sick and imprisoned
- Burying the dead

It is important to notice two things: that all of the works are directed toward what we should do for others, and that "others" includes all people, whether they profess belief in Christ or not. They are works of mercy because they express the love that God has toward all his people and shows us that we are to be his instruments, as well as emphasizing that we have been and continue to be the recipients of his mercy. They express the arrival of the kingdom of God.

The last thing that I wish to point out before offering a brief discussion of the most salient aspects of the works is that they are grounded in prayer and faithfulness. We are not called to be social workers but rather disciples of the Lord and followers of his way. If we are not rooted in the faith when we act, we will fall prey to pragmatic opportunism and soon come to believe that all on earth depends upon us and our will. On the other hand, if we do not act and only pray, we will become abstracting theologians, separated and aloof from the world. It seems to me that one way to solve Bonhoeffer's dilemma is to join our acts of mercy to lives of prayer and resist the temptation to compartmentalize our commitments into distinct aspects and divide ourselves among the different spheres of interactions.

I tend to think of the spiritual works of mercy as divided into three groups of actions. The first two, instructing and advising, seem to speak most to our call to be truthful. They access our intellects and call for a great deal of courage because I think we most need to instruct and advise when the ignorant do not recognize their ignorance. Just speaking for myself, that is when I am most in need of merciful interventions—and I am often not grateful for the lessons others have tried to teach me until much later, if then. We are called to speak the truth even when no one wishes to hear the truth and even if we suffer for it.

If the first two spiritual works of mercy address our intellect and truth telling, the second two call on our emotions and empathy. To console and to comfort requires us to be *with* those who are suffering, to enter into their suffering with them. Comfort and solace do not relieve the pain of loss or victimhood but reach across the divide that the pain causes: grief and suffering isolate those who are consumed by them. They are alone in a close, dark place and have lost the ability to see or feel beyond the pain. This was the experience of Mary I wrote of earlier. At the death of Lazarus she had nothing left but pain and anger and could not be touched. These are not times when a detached therapist is needed. We are called to be there inside that pain, to take it on and in so doing connect ourselves with the victims. We are called to wait and be ready to touch them when they are ready to be touched, to suffer with them and help bring them back.

The last two spiritual works change the focus a little bit. With these two works, we are the victims and we are called to bear the wrongs patiently and to forgive those who have wronged us. I suppose it is inevitable that we will suffer if we live the way we are called, but I think these two works are asking us to move beyond ourselves and focus upon the perpetrators of injustice and evil. Often when I have been harmed unjustly I see only myself as a victim and nothing else—my concern is revenge or justification, or else I simply want to brood and sulk. What I think we are called to in these works is to relinquish our desire for the violence of revenge and replace it with patient suffering, and we must forgive.

Forgiveness poses a special problem for me because it is not qualified by what I want. I want my forgiveness of an evildoer to be deserved; I want the perpetrator to recognize that she or he needs forgiveness, and furthermore to ask for it. But that is not what this work involves. I must forgive even when it is not deserved and even when it is not requested. I suppose there is a certain justice in this, since I expect God to forgive me my sins even when I do not ask and even though I do not deserve it. As a matter of fact, as I think about it, I am not sure that any of us ever deserves forgiveness, either divine or from each other. If I knowingly and intentionally harm someone, I can't think of anything I could do that would make forgiveness something I deserve. Rather, forgiveness is always a gift to those who have no possible claim to it. This does not seem to be much of a problem for me when I forgive those whom I love, but it is very difficult to forgive strangers or those I don't like. Again, these are works that can be done consistently only with frequent practice.

The corporal works of mercy focus more on the material needs of God's people. It is obvious that the first four of these works are concerned with the poor and outcast of the world. The first three of the corporal works address the basic needs all of us have, and we are told to feed, shelter, and clothe those who are in need. Once again, these works imply that we know who is needy; we must not only live among the destitute—in fact we already do—but we must force ourselves to become aware of them. Our eyes need to be trained to see, and our ears to hear, and that is the first task we must accomplish before we can be instruments of God's mercy. I speak as a bourgeois intellectual of the kind that Orwell sneered at. I am comfortable in my isolation, and I am frightened of the poor, probably because I fear they will steal from me but also because I am embarrassed by my selfishness and wealth. When it occurs to me to give to the poor, it is almost always an afterthought, and I give pocket change, crumbs from my excess. More often I am hypocritical. When a drunk approaches me on the street and asks for a dollar to get something to eat, I deny it to him because I know he'll use the money to buy wine. It never occurs to me to go and buy a sandwich and give it to him. Thus I can preserve the illusion that I am helping a brother while I ignore him.

I don't think this is uncommon for those of us who have been lucky enough to garner some wealth. But this separation of ourselves from those who are starving, naked, and homeless speaks to our valuing our possessions and comfort more than the people of God. It helps us to see ourselves as special cases whose status needs preservation and whose comfortable way of life must be protected. When I value my money and goods more than I value others, violence in protecting these things follows naturally. When Jesus says, "You have the poor with you always" (John 12:8), I don't think he is describing an intractable social problem regarding the distribution of wealth. I believe, rather, that he is telling us that as church we are to be living with the poor of the world always, that it is impermissible for us to separate ourselves from them and be blind and nonresponsive to their needs.

Visiting the sick and burying the dead are akin to the spiritual works of comforting and consoling. We are being asked to enter into a recognition of mortality by doing what we can for those whose bodies are suffering or who have been abandoned in death—for we believe that the dead are not gone from us. In addition to the comfort we can provide to the ill and the dead, we need to learn about dying in order to die well. I wrote above about my fears regarding dying and death, fears that I believe are common ones. If we are to recognize and acknowledge Jesus's lordship and power over death, we need to be companions to those who are dying. Those who are alone who are sick need to see, feel, and hear tangible expressions of love. And the same is true also for those who have died, though it seems strange to say so. Our burying of the dead is a gift of love for them, and our mourning of their passing connects us to them. No child of God should be forgotten. The sick and the dying have called out to the Lord in their fear and pain, and we are meant to be God's response to that summons and his blessing to them. Again, this should not be a detached and therapeutic intervention but rather a joining with them in their suffering and a willingness to be with them and take care of them when no one else will.

I have saved visiting the imprisoned for last because in many ways it is the most difficult of the works. We should ask ourselves who are the imprisoned, and the answer will be the worst of society. A fair number of those who are convicted are sociopaths, killers, rapists, child molesters—evildoers without conscience or remorse. We are told to visit them in the same sense as we are to visit the sick. If I am uncomfortable around the poor because of unfounded fears that they will harm me, I will be very scared around those who clearly would. No one would seem to deserve my condemnation and scorn more than the criminals in jail.

But this is not how we are called to react. Our response to the evildoers we see and fear in our communities is to be one of love, forgiveness, and comfort. The murderer and the rapist and the child molester are no less children of God because of their crimes and are not loved any the less by God because of their sins. Their actions may be repugnant, but they should be loved and called back. We are asked to enter into union with the imprisoned in the same way that we are called to join with the sick, the poor, the grieving, and the suffering. In a related way the imprisoned are also dying, even though they may not realize it. We must not separate ourselves from them either or regard them from a position of aloof superiority. They are our brothers and sisters, and we are called to be the instruments of God's mercy to them as well.

Here now we have arrived at the end of this small journey, and we must return to the beginning of the book. In the first chapter I spoke disparagingly about St. Augustine's discussion of inward dispositions. It is important to recall that my objection was directed primarily at the way Augustine divided our inward, spiritual dispositions from our actions. The result of dividing ourselves in this way is that violence and war can be justified as actions of faithfulness and love. None of this is possible. But I want to stress that Augustine is correct in the emphasis he placed on our inward dispositions—he erred only in the division. Our inward dispositions are linked to our actions in such a way that one must affect the other. Our faith and love of God direct our actions to be loving and peacemaking, and our faith-filled actions reinforce our call to discipleship and bring us closer to God. The answer to the Hitler question cannot come from armchair theoreticians of the geopolitical. It is only through prayer and our daily practices that we allow ourselves to be formed into disciples of the Lord and his peacemakers.

A friend who read an earlier draft of this book commented that one of his disappointments is the lack of joy in what I have written, that what I have spoken about is almost unremittingly bleak. I suppose that is due, at least in part, to the subject matter, though, as I have said, I have a tendency and temptation not only to view my joyful brothers and sisters with suspicion but also to stress the passion at the expense of the resurrection. Nonetheless, what I have written about, especially in these last two chapters, is joyful.

Joy should not be confused with blissful happiness or having an easy time of it—at least, that is not what I understand joy to be. Rather, I think we feel joy the most when we have found ourselves and have good work to do, and when we realize that the good work we have to do arises from finding ourselves. The only message that counts in the end is that we find ourselves in the love of God, and our work is to try to love God in return and express that love to him and to each other. As Dorothy Day has written:

> When one is in love, one cannot conceive of not being in love. Life seems dull and dead to contemplate without this vital emotion. . . . And you will agree with me that the desire for sacrifice comes with love. . . . Yes, love, great love—and who wishes to be mediocre in love?—brings with it a desire for suffering. The love of God can be so overwhelming that it wishes to do everything for the Beloved, to endure hunger, cold, sleeplessness in an ecstasy of zeal and enthusiasm. There is a love so great that the Beloved is all and oneself nothing, and this realization, leading to humility, a real joyful humility which desires to do the least, the meanest, the hardest as well as the most revolting tasks, to crush the pride of self, to abandon oneself fully. (171–72)

While I am not sure that great love brings with it a *desire* to suffer, I do think that great love does not count the cost and that the cost of loving greatly may well include suffering. That does not diminish the joy of love, as the Beloved showed us when he proclaimed the kingdom.

Works Cited

Arendt, Hannah. *Eichmann in Jerusalem*. New York: Penguin Books, 1992.

Augustine. *City of God*. Tr. Marcus Dods. New York: Random House, 1950.

Augustine. *Contra Faustum Manichaeum*. In *Nicene and Post-Nicene Fathers of the Christian Church*. Vol. 4. Ed. Philip Schaff (with emendations by the author). Grand Rapids: Eerdmans, 1979 (1890).

Babiarz, Liz. "Maryland Hospices Get High Marks." December 19, 2002. Capital News Service. www.journalism.umd.edu/cns/wire/2002–editions/.

Bainton, Roland. *Christian Attitudes toward War and Peace*. Nashville: Abingdon Press, 1960.

Bethge, Eberhard. *Dietrich Bonhoeffer,* rev. ed. Minneapolis: Fortress Press, 2000.

bin Laden, Osama. "Letter to America." November 24, 2002. http://observer.guardian.co.uk/worldview/story/0,11581,845725,00.html.

Bonhoeffer, Dietrich. *Letters and Papers from Prison*. Ed. Eberhard Bethge. Tr. Reginald Fuller. New York: Macmillan, 1967.

Bonhoeffer, Dietrich. *The Cost of Discipleship*. Tr. R. H. Fuller. New York: Macmillan, 1963.

Borg, Marcus. "Endorsement of Every Church a Peace Church." 2005. www.ecapc.org/endorsements.asp.

Buber, Martin. *Israel and the World: Essays in a Time of Crisis*. New York: Schocken Books, 1963.

Catechism of the Catholic Church. New York: Doubleday, 1995.

Charter of the United Nations. www.un.org/aboutun/charter/.

Day, Dorothy. *From Union Square to Rome*. Silver Spring, MD: Preservation of the Faith Press, 1938.

de Beauvoir, Simone. "Must We Burn Sade?" In de Beauvoir, *The Marquis de Sade*. Ed. Paul Dinnage. Tr. Annette Michelson. New York: Grove Press, 1953.

Elshtain, Jean Bethke. *Just War against Terrorism*. New York: Basic Books, 2003.

Gadamer, Hans Georg. *The Enigma of Health*. Tr. Jason Gaiger and Nicholas Walker. Stanford, CA: Stanford University Press, 1996.

Goldhagen, Daniel Jonah. *Hitler's Willing Executioners*. New York: Alfred A. Knopf, 1996.

Hauerwas, Stanley. *Performing the Faith*. Grand Rapids: Brazos Press, 2004.

Holmes, Robert L. *On War and Morality*. Princeton: Princeton University Press, 1984.

Johnson, James Turner. *Can Modern War Be Just?* New Haven: Yale University Press, 1984.

Jones, L. Gregory. *Embodying Forgiveness*. Grand Rapids: Eerdmans, 1995.

Levinas, Emmanuel. *Difficult Freedom*. Tr. Sean Hand. Baltimore: Johns Hopkins University Press, 1997.

Orwell, George. "Reflections on Gandhi." In *The Orwell Reader*. New York: Harcourt Brace Jovanovich, 1956, 328–35.

———*My Country Right or Left*. In *The Collected Essays, Journalism and Letters of George Orwell*. Vol. 2. Ed. Sonia Orwell and Ian Angress. London: Seeker and Warburg, 1968.

Rawls, John. *The Law of Peoples*. Cambridge: Harvard University Press, 2001

Slane, Craige J. *Bonhoeffer as Martyr*. Grand Rapids: Brazos Press, 2004

Tertullian. *De Corona*. In *The Ante-Nicene* Fathers. Vol. III. Ed. Alexander Roberts and James Donaldson (with emendations by the author). Grand Rapids: Eerdmans, 1900

Thomas Aquinas. *The Summa Theologica*. Ed. Daniel J. Sullican. Chicago: Encyclopedia Brittanica, 1952

United States Conference of Catholic Bishops. *Challenge of Peace: God's Promise and Our Response*. Washington, D.C.: United States Catholic Conference, 1983

Walzer, Michael. *Just and Unjust Wars*, 3rd edition. New York; Basic Books, 2000